SAS

MILITARY ILLUSTRATED

SAS

SPECIAL FORCES IN ACTION
WRITTEN BY STEPHEN BULL

SERIES EDITOR: TIM NEWARK
COLOUR PLATES BY RICHARD HOOK

Current titles
Marine
Stormtrooper
Rifleman
Highlander
Ranger
SAS

Future titles
Paratrooper
Commando

First published in 2000 in Great Britain
by Publishing News Ltd

UK editorial office:
Military Illustrated, 39 Store Street,
London WC1E 7DB, Great Britain

Stephen Bull has asserted his moral right
to be identified as the author of this work.

ISBN 1-903040-05-1

Designed by Glenn Howard

Printed and bound in Singapore under
the supervision of M.R.M. Graphics Ltd,
Winslow, Buckinghamshire

CONTENTS

BIRTH OF THE SAS

One of the world's most famous regiments was born almost by accident. The Commandos, arguably Britain's first Special Forces troops, had been in existence only a short time when it was decided that No 2 Commando should be converted to parachute troops. In November 1940, the new unit received the somewhat obscure temporary name of the 11th Special Air Service Battalion. Six months later, this title would be dropped and the parachute arm was developed into Parachute Battalions, and finally into the Parachute Regiment. Yet the idea that it was possible to drop small units of experimental Special Forces from aircraft, and that such troops might be known as a Special Air Service lived on.

In the spring of 1941, members of the Commando Layforce found themselves inactive, and in danger of disbandment, in North Africa. Since officers and men had volunteered for the Commandos in order to see active service, it was not surprising that some of them should seek a new aggressive outlet. According to regimental lore, a consignment of parachutes bound for India was unexpectedly unloaded at Alexandria. With the encouragement of Brigadier Laycock, members of No 8 Commando, who were then based at Kabrit, began jumping from an elderly Vickers Valencia aircraft. The result was disappointing, second-rate equipment and inexperience led to a spate of injuries. One of the jumpers was a tall and hitherto less than successful Scots Guards reservist, Lieutenant David Stirling. As he left the aircraft, his parachute had caught on its tail, ripped, and then flapped inefficiently as he dropped at alarming speed towards the ground. The impact injured his back and left his legs temporarily useless.

Stirling, widely acknowledged as both the founder and driving force behind the SAS, had an established military pedigree – he was one of six children of General Archibald Stirling of Keir and his wife Margaret Fraser, the daughter of Baron Lovat. Even so, he did not appear a natural-born leader.

His childhood was restricted by a speech impediment and a reputation for sulkiness. His early life was a patchwork of adventure, indecision, and irresponsibility. After schooling at Ampleforth, he went up to Cambridge, only to be sent down again for a variety of offences. He then decided to become an artist and went to Paris. This proved unsuccessful and he returned to Cambridge for a while before deciding to become an architect. Quitting this profession before it even took off, he began training for an assault on Mount Everest by climbing in the Alps and Rocky Mountains. Distracted from the Everest project, he then had a spell as a cowboy before further climbing and walking in Colorado and along the Rio Grande. At the outbreak of the Second World War, he returned to Britain. He was only just 24. As a dreamer and a rebel he would not fit in with either the Scots Guards or the Commandos, so much so that a board of officers considered whether he should face a court martial.

According to Stirling's later recollections of his parachute injury, the ensuing period of bed rest turned out to be 'a good thing', since it gave him time to ponder the shortcomings of Commando warfare, North African topography, and the Special Service Brigade in general. His musings resulted in the conclusion that to be effective, other than as an advanced landing or beach-holding operation, Special Forces would need to be organised in smaller groups. These very small units could be parachuted or otherwise inserted onto enemy lines of communication where they would cause havoc, without the need for expensive resupply, and have a disproportionate effect on a campaign. Controversially, it was suggested that such troops should be answerable directly to the commander-in-chief, not to any intermediate formation. North Africa seemed to offer special potential for such action in 1941. Axis supply lines were long, airfields were vulnerable, and relatively few men were available for the guarding of rear areas. The rugged

long desert flank, south of the warring armies, might be invulnerable to a division, but could be just the terrain to harbour a few dozen determined men.

It was remarkable that the main points of Stirling's apparently madcap schemes should have been accepted by General Auchinleck, but accepted they were, and Stirling was promoted and given leave to recruit five officers and 60 men for the purpose. The name picked out of the air for this group was L Detachment, 1st Special Air Service Brigade. This was a deliberate deception, another unit was already christened K Detachment, and it was all calculated to give any observant enemy the impression that the British had a complete airborne brigade in Egypt. In these details may lie the real reason for the formation of the SAS. For though the unit was ostensibly secret, it was featured on cinema film within months, and formed the subject for a set of official photographs. It may well have been the case that Middle East Headquarters thought that the troublesome

Stirling actually had no chance of success, but that his efforts might be a valuable distraction and propaganda tool for use against the enemy. If this was the case, then events were soon to take a very unexpected turn.

Stirling soon found the troops he needed. Amongst the officers were Lieutenant Jock Lewes, a Welsh oarsman who was put in charge of parachute training, Captain R.B. 'Paddy' Mayne, a pugnacious Irish sportsman, and Lieutenant Tom Langton of the Irish Guards. The non-commissioned officers included Sergeant Pat Riley, an American citizen later to be promoted Regimental Sergeant Major of the SAS, and Sergeant Jim Almonds, formerly of the Coldstream Guards. Many of the other ranks came from Layforce and some of them were ex-Scots Guardsmen. The detachment was not a regiment, nor was it yet entitled to any special badge or uniform, but was soon made proficient in demolitions, air drops, and arduous long range marches, all of which were seen as vital to their likely operational tasks. The SAS camp promptly gained a reputation as a place best avoided, somewhere that even Eric Newby of the SBS regarded as 'not for the chicken-hearted'. Amongst other pieces of training, the novice saboteurs 'attacked' the RAF base at Heliopolis and attached paper labels to the aircraft. They also 'raided' a New Zealand camp, stealing, amongst other more practical items, a piano.

ACTION IN THE DESERT

The first real SAS mission came in November 1941 (the Regiment still regards its official birthday as 17 November). Although it followed Stirling's prescription for a long range strike by a small group of parachutists against enemy airfields, the first mission was intelligently planned as a support to, and diversion from, the general 8th Army offensive Operation Crusader. The other Special Forces attack, mounted simultaneously with the main effort, was Lieutenant Colonel Geoffrey Keyes'

The Duke of Gloucester visits parachutists in training, Kabrit, North Africa, 1941. He examines a drop container. On the ground nearby may be seen rifles, Thompson sub-machine guns, and a Bren. David Stirling's Special Forces scheme was born here.

SAS parachute training, North Africa, November 1941. The men jump off the back of moving trucks and attempt to land safely, a form of training that David Sutherland would describe as 'exquisitely painful'.

Commando raid on Rommel's headquarters. Keyes' heroic failure earned him a posthumous Victoria Cross. The men of No 11 Commando had great difficulty landing on the coast due to a heavy swell, but Keyes and a couple of others succeeded in penetrating to the villa only to have the surprise ruined by a shot fired during a struggle with a sentry. In an exchange of fire and grenades, Keyes was shot dead. Unfortunately, Rommel was not there, but in Rome at the time.

The SAS contribution was the landing of 55 men by parachute, in five groups each led by an officer. Stirling, Mayne, and Lewes took a group each as did Bonnington and McGonigal. These were to march from their drop zones approximately 12 miles northwards, observe the enemy airfields around Timini and Gazala, then fall upon them under cover of darkness and destroy the aircraft with incendiaries and explosives. By 16 November, winds were gusting dangerously fast, and Stirling was forced to make a difficult judgment as to the viability of the operation. Having decided to proceed, conditions in the air were found to be even worse than expected.

Cloud, sandstorms, and enemy activity all hampered the approach, as was recorded by a veteran of Stirling's party: 'The pilot straightened up and rose… to 500 feet. The green light had come on. As we stood up and got ready, Jock said the pilot was not exactly sure of our position because of the atrocious weather and the activities of the anti-aircraft gunners. He added that the wind speed was force nine… Then suddenly we were given the signal and the whole stick jumped together. I felt a terrific tug as my parachute opened and then I was swinging in comparative quietness except for the wind howling through my rigging lines. I could see two other parachutes which seemed to be drifting away at a vast speed. As it was impossible to see the ground I kept my legs braced, but when I hit the desert I suffered a tremendous jolt right through my body… I found myself being dragged across the desert floor at more than 30 mph by the wind. Vainly I banged my quick release box… to jettison my parachute… I managed to roll clear just as it flew off into the air, never to be seen again.'

Stirling's group had a lucky escape and managed to assemble on the ground, only to find most of its supply containers were missing. With little explosives, food or weaponry, it was as much as they could do to extricate themselves back to the point south of the Trig el Abd, where, much later, the vehicles of the Long Range Desert Group rendezvoused to collect them. Most were not so lucky, some were killed, others captured.

Lieutenant Charles Bonnington's Bristol Bombay was piloted by Warrant Officer Charlie West. All went well for a while until the plane hit a storm, lost direction, descended to obtain orientation, and was promptly hit by flak. The port engine was shot out and the instrument panel shattered. West turned the craft back on what he believed to be the correct heading, but soon made a forced landing. As Sergeant Ernie Bond related: 'The weather improved as the night wore on and just before dawn we took a patrol out to try to get our bearings. We were pretty sure that we were in friendly territory but surprise, surprise, we came across an Italian position. There was a short sharp skirmish

Above, **Target of opportunity – smashed German 88 mm flak gun. War Office picture released to press November, 1942.**

Opposite, **Captain (finally Major General) David Lloyd Owen of the Long Range Desert Group (LRDG) pictured with a 30 cwt truck outside the Farouk Hotel, Siwa Oasis, November 1941. As an LRDG patrol leader, Lloyd Owen served with distinction as a combat taxi driver to the SAS,** **and later as operational planner. His typically eccentric outfit includes Service Dress cap, still with the badge of the Queen's Regiment, scarf, battle dress blouse, sweater, and khaki drill trousers.** ***IWM HU 25299***

Corporal James McDiarmid,
SAS, in typical desert attire.
Arab head dress is worn with
veil scarf and a leather jerkin.
IWM E 21348

and we took one very frightened Eytie back to the aircraft. By the time we returned, Charlie West had discovered that his compass was jammed by a piece of shrapnel. So we must have been trundling round in a bloody great circle the night before… We got back into the plane in a hell of a rush. The poor bloody Eytie was jammed on top of the fuel tank and told to sit still.'

Charlie West then managed to get the craft back into the sky, but was again engaged by flak. Another hit forced a second emergency landing, far rougher than the first, and the co-pilot was killed and others injured. Bonnington's team were now taken prisoner by the Germans, and though at least one escape was attempted, Bonnington, Bond, and others would spend the remainder of the war in captivity after only one abortive mission. Paddy Mayne's group had succeeded in jumping, but had two men injured. Lewes headed back with eight, one man missing, another left behind with a broken leg. Eoin McGonigal and his entire team were missing, presumed dead.

After 10 days waiting, Y2 patrol of the LRDG (Long Range Desert Group) spotted Mayne, Stirling, and a few men walking towards them. In all, only 22 escaped. More than half of the fledgling SAS had been sacrificed in an operation which failed to inflict any damage on the enemy. Operation Crusader, which had been launched as planned on 18 November, was itself enveloped by *Afrika Korps* counter- attacks and dissolved into a confused armoured battle, although Rommel was eventually pushed out of Cyrenaica.

LONG RANGE RAIDERS

Despite this failure, it was to Auckinleck's credit that the SAS idea was not only kept alive but allowed to develop after such a spectacular false start. Almost immediately Stirling agreed with officers of the LRDG that parachuting was unnecessarily dangerous, and that if the driving and navigational skills of the LRDG could be relied

upon to extricate them, then they could also be used to provide a 'taxi' service to the targets. So it was, hard on the heels of some very successful LRDG patrols, that the SAS was again committed to action. The December attacks, all launched from LRDG patrols, were planned as a series of rapid blows from the newly acquired base at Jalo against Axis air power. On 8 December, Stirling and Mayne accompanied S1 patrol to Sirte and Tamet. On 9 December, Lewes left with T2 for Aghelia. And soon after, Lieutenant Bill Fraser and his party went for Agedabia. Opportunity allowing, these and other targets could also be hit again later.

Patrol S1 split up when discovered by an Italian reconnaissance aircraft, and though Stirling found Sirte airfield abandoned, Mayne had better hunting during the night at Tamet. The spectacular results have become the stuff of legend, as was reported by RSM Bennett: 'Paddy spotted this Nissen hut… and sneaked up… dragged the bloody door open and was letting rip with his tommy gun. Screams from inside and the lights went out. The buggers inside soon started firing. Paddy put a couple of guys on the ground to keep the Krauts' heads down and the rest of us went after the planes. We got through our bombs pretty quick.' Mayne discovered that he had less bombs than there were planes, so he climbed into the cockpit of one of the

David Stirling, towards the centre of the group in service dress cap, with a mixed SAS and LRDG patrol pictured at Bir Hachim, May 1942. SAS men Reg Seekings and Johnny Cooper are the two figures foreground left in Arab headgear. The vehicle bears the winged dagger insignia. *IWM HU 69650*

others and smashed the controls. One account which has entered folklore has it that he wrenched away part of the instrument panel and carried it off as a souvenir.

Jock Lewes' raiders were dropped by Lieutenant Morris of the LRDG near Aghelia with a view to attacking planes on the airfield. There were none, but the SAS succeeded in using their bombs on a truck park. Meanwhile, Morris drove off in the direction of Mersa Brega and attacked an enemy convoy at close range, stirring up a hornet's nest, but mining the road behind to impede a rapid pursuit. Fraser's attack was the most significant as he and a handful of men were able to penetrate Agedabia Field without detection, plant a large number of bombs, and then escape in the confusion as they exploded. A vast number of enemy aircraft were claimed as a result of these raids; even the Italian official history admits that the better part of 30 were lost. The triumph was only marred by an RAF attack on Fraser's party on the return journey, resulting in the death of two men.

Before December was out, the raiders were back again. At Sirte, Stirling failed to reach any aircraft and had a narrow escape when an Italian sentry's rifle malfunctioned. Remarkably, Mayne hit Tamet a second time, actually destroying some aircraft which had been brought in to replace

Captain (later Lieutenant Colonel) John Haselden disguised as an Arab making contact with a patrol. Haselden was a former cotton broker and fluent Arabic speaker who acted as a guide on various Special Forces operations. Careful reconnaissance and local knowledge was invaluable to the SAS.

those blown up only a few days earlier. Fraser and Lewes were taken by Morris and T2 patrol to attack the strips at Nofalia and Ras Lanuf (which the British called 'Marble Arch' due to the monument Mussolini had built there). Lewes found and attacked aircraft at Nofalia, but was discovered due to the premature detonation of a bomb and was forced to beat a hasty retreat. His group managed to rejoin his LRDG rescuers, but was then subjected to air attack by a Messerschmitt. The LRDG report takes up the story: 'Shortly after two Stukas joined the chase and the attack was kept up by relays of aircraft for most of the morning. Although there was not enough cover to hide the men, still less the trucks, the patrol had only one casualty, Lt Lewes being killed, and all but one of the vehicles burnt out.'

During the attacks, the trucks became widely separated, and although Morris and part of the patrol managed to get back to Jalo in the one roadworthy vehicle, some of the LRDG and Corporal White of the SAS were stranded in the desert 200 miles from safety. They began the gruelling march back, but White fell out, explaining that he intended to attempt to capture a truck. His comrades realised his feet were already in too poor a state and that he was probably going to sacrifice himself to allow the others to escape, which they eventually did, with aid from Senussi tribesmen. Captain Fraser's SAS men spent six days near 'Marble Arch' waiting for the doomed transport, and they too were forced to come back on foot, a journey which took eight horrendous days.

The destruction of a total of about 90 aircraft during late 1941 had been arduous, and not without setbacks, the death of Jock Lewes being arguably the most significant. Yet it was an almost unprecedented success. So it was that whilst the army fell back in front of Rommel and regrouped, Stirling and Mayne received Distinguished Service Orders, promotions to Major and Captain respectively, and permission for expansion of the unit by a further 46 all ranks. The next important operation saw the SAS co-operating with the Special Boat Section, skilled Commando swimmers and canoeists.

On 17 January, 1942, a group of 12 SAS, accompanied by Captain Duncan and Corporal Barr of the Special Boat Squadron, were transported across the desert by the LRDG to Bouerat on the coast. Here, Captain Duncan was to have launched his boat and attack tankers in the port, but there were none nearby, and in any case the canoe had suffered damage. The wireless truck was also lost to air attack. The group had to

content itself with planting devices in the radio station, on fuel bowsers, and in warehouses before retiring. The report on the mission claimed: 'it was with great satisfaction that the party later felt the tremors of explosions and watched the desert sky turn red with flames of burning petrol'. It may have been this result which encouraged raids on the more significant target of Benghazi.

The first attempt to limpet mine ships there in March 1942 was unsuccessful owing to poor sea conditions, but the raiders managed to withdraw without mishap, whilst Mayne and two men attacked and destroyed a number of planes on Becra Airfield. On the next visit to Benghazi,

An LRDG Chevrolet truck, ready to leave Cairo for active service, May 1942. The front seat passenger mans an Italian Breda machine gun, whilst a Lewis gun can be fired from the rear. The driver has an SMLE rifle handy in a bracket beside his seat. Other details visible include a cylindrical water condenser mounted near the driver, and sand channels fitted to the rear compartment.

Stirling was in distinguished company, being with Fitzroy Maclean and Randolph Churchill, and it was Maclean who detailed their exploits on this mission in *Eastern Approaches*. According to Maclean, the SAS party was just outside Benghazi, driving a car disguised to look like a German vehicle, when stopped by Italians. Maclean told them they were staff officers, and they drove on into the town. The car was now malfunctioning, and Stirling became convinced that he was being followed, so he drove into a side street, with the intention of destroying the vehicle. Having prepared the car with an explosive charge, they walked away, only to run into another Italian as an air raid warning sounded. They were informed that there were no British ground forces in the area. Since they obviously had not been compromised, they rapidly returned to the car and removed the explosives.

The farce continued when the SAS men reached the harbour, pretending that their collapsible boat was luggage and that they were looking for a hotel. It looked as though they were going to succeed getting into the water and were struggling to inflate their craft, when they were confronted, as Maclean relates: "'Chi va la ?' he challenged. 'Militari!' I shouted back. There was a pause and we resumed pumping. But the sentry was still suspicious. 'What are you doing over there ?'

An SAS fighting patrol jeep near Gabes. The passenger mans a Browning .50 calibre heavy machine gun and carries a pistol. Vickers 'K' guns are fitted for the driver and for use from the rear. Fuel and water make up much of the heavy load.

he inquired. "Nothing to do with you," I answered, with a show of assurance which I was far from feeling. After that there was silence. Meanwhile the boat remained flat… it had got punctured… There was nothing for it but to go and get another. Once again we got safely through the wire and down to the water's edge, but only to find that the second boat, like the first, was uninflatable.'

On the way back, Stirling's party was challenged yet again, and again managed to bluff their way out of the situation. It was a stirring but ultimately fruitless performance, yet it contributed to Stirling's new nickname 'the Phantom Major'. Maclean and Churchill were subsequently injured in a road crash, from which Stirling escaped with only a cracked wrist bone.

SAS EXPANDED

It has been argued, perhaps correctly, that it was Randolph Churchill's influence with his father, the Prime Minister, that allowed Stirling to expand the SAS during 1942. In any case, in addition to the further 40 men which Auckinleck had sanctioned, a detachment of Free French parachutists under Commandant Bergé was brought into Stirling's order of battle. These would feature prominently in plans for wide-ranging raids to be carried out in mid-June 1942, mounted against Axis air power to help safeguard British convoys. The ambitious scheme would see Stirling and Mayne return to the Benghazi area, whilst French patrols were directed to Derna, Berka, and Heraklion on Crete.

An unusual feature of these attacks was the use of half a dozen fake German soldiers under Captain Herbert Buck, who would smooth the path of the French SAS raiders onto the most difficult targets. Some of Buck's men were German-speaking Palestinian Jews, two being supposedly anti-Nazi German prisoners of war who had volunteered for the task. At first, all went well, and the counterfeit Germans were even able to secure the necessary passwords from real German soldiers *en route* to

Derna. Later one of the trucks driven by a German called Brückner began to malfunction, and Brückner went off to try and find tools. Moments later the Frenchmen of Lieutenant Jordan's group were surrounded by German soldiers – Brückner had betrayed them, but they were not about to give up without a fight. Shots were exchanged and the truck exploded. Some of the SAS managed to escape only to find that other parts of the plan had also been betrayed and frustrated.

Bergé's patrol got onto Crete by using inflatable boats launched from the submarine *Triton*. After a scare caused by an alert sentry, they managed to cut their way through the perimeter fence of Heraklion Airfield, and attached bombs to over 20 aircraft and stores. On their return to the beach to rendezvous with their transport, they were betrayed, but nevertheless tried to fight their way out. Some men, including Bergé himself, were wounded and captured. Only two men managed to escape.

Stirling, Mayne and Jaquier had better success. Stirling attacked the field at Benina, taking with him only Reg Seekings and Johnny Cooper, original L Detachment stalwarts, his assault being planned to follow a diversionary air raid. Entering stealthily, they found the hangars well stocked with Messerschmitts and Stukas, and discovered the bonus of a large fuel store not hitherto identified. About 60 Lewis bombs were placed, and for good

Semi formal SAS uniform as worn in the latter part of the campaign in North Africa. Note the field service cap worn with cloth winged dagger badge.

Corporal Sillitoe, SAS, after a 100-mile walk back from behind enemy lines in North Africa, 1942. Failing to meet his comrades at a desert rendezvous, Sillitoe trekked without food, his only water being what he was able to drink from a puddle. His swollen and blistered feet are still bandaged several days later. *IWM E19781*

Next page, David Stirling, standing in duffle coat, next to Lieutenant McDonald and his jeep patrol. Vickers and Browning machine guns are much in evidence as are the cylindrical condensers fitted to the fronts of the vehicles in order to save precious water. *IWM E 21338*

measure Stirling threw a grenade into the guard house as the party made their escape. He would later admit that the grenade was a 'show of bravado', but it was certainly the icing on the cake as the planes began to explode just as they were passing the perimeter.

Mayne found the field at Berka better guarded, and only managed to plant bombs on a fuel store before a full-scale alert made him beat a hasty retreat. Pursued by enemy vehicles, Mayne took the risky decision to split his party, but everyone made it clear. Later, Stirling and Mayne actually returned to Benina in the hope of seeing the damage inflicted, and to bomb another petrol store. On their return, they were pursued by a German truck and accidentally blew their own vehicle to pieces with one of their own bombs. The damage caused in this series of raids was considerable, but the blooding of the French, and the experiment with 'turned' prisoners had proved expensive.

Into the desert. Contrary to popular belief, not all deserts are seas of sand, many consist of hills and broken rock. All are dry and barren, but can be cold at night. War Office picture issued to press January 1943.

During the summer of 1942, attacks were launched on air fields in the vicinity of Sidi Barrani, El Dhaba, and Bagush, and it was at this time that SAS tactics underwent a minor revolution. More vehicles were now available, and Stirling managed to acquire 15 Jeeps as well as support vehicles. The Jeeps were fitted with Vickers K aircraft guns fore and aft. Very quickly it occurred to Stirling that with the Jeeps the time-consuming and dangerous process of fusing and placing individual bombs could become superfluous. As he put it: 'There we were with guns aboard which were designed for the RAF to shoot down aircraft in the air – why couldn't we do just that from the ground and keep the bombs in reserve? Paddy [Mayne] was all for it and we decided simply to drive onto the field and shoot the beggars up. It was amazingly easy.'

After an experiment at Bagush, Stirling decided to try out the new tactics on a major night raid against Sidi Haneish, where vital JU 52 transport planes were kept in quantity. To the surprise of the attackers, the airfield lit up to allow a plane to land as they approached. The opportunity was seized and the Jeeps fanned out to spray the field with bullets from a total of 68 Vickers machine guns. Raking backwards and forwards along the ranks of aircraft put many out of action, and started several fires. Mayne, being something of a perfectionist as well as an enthusiast, got out of his vehicle and put a bomb on a plane that was proving stubborn. Yet by now the enemy had begun to return fire, and had mortars in action. So Stirling ordered the retreat and, at a cost of one man killed and three Jeeps put out of action, the raiders made their escape. Another man was lost on the return, but about 40 German transport planes were destroyed.

Successes such as Sidi Haneish influenced high command to try and integrate SAS activity into set piece land campaigns. For a short period, SAS vehicles were allotted to the area immediately behind the enemy lines, in an attempt to disrupt Axis transport around the El Alamein line.

An SAS man helps to load mortar rounds into a landing craft, invasion of Sicily, 1943. Note the SAS parachute wings worn on his right upper arm, and the use of a tank crew holster worn low on his right thigh.

Later, and much more dangerously, the SAS were committed to a very large-scale raid on Benghazi during September 1942, in what Stirling would call a 'thundering herd' of almost 100 vehicles. The result was disaster.

Sheer numbers and an alert enemy meant that they ran into trouble even before they reached the target. As one of the raiders put it: 'They opened up with everything they'd got. The extraordinary thing was that they scored very few hits. Just as well because sitting on our explosives we would have disappeared in a big bang. We were told to get out of it, every man for himself, in Jeep and lorry as best we could. There was a great deal of confusion, backing and filling of trucks trying to turn round. Shot and stuff flying all over the place without anybody lost except one Jeep, hit in the petrol tank, which went up in flames, adding to the already illuminated scene. We headed out of it, having achieved nothing at all; a complete fiasco… At break of day we were all haring hell for leather… they got the fighters up, strafing, bombing… For the whole of the day we lay up under camouflage netting. The rest of the force had a fearful dusting about a mile or two west of us which went on all day, machine gunning and bombing.'

The ill-fated Benghazi raid cost the SAS about a quarter of its strength for no result. Casualties were made all the worse by the distance that the wounded had to be carried back in the remaining transport. Even so, Stirling was invited to meet the Prime Minister soon afterwards, and during September 1942 the SAS was accorded official regimental status, ceasing to be a detachment, and becoming 1st SAS Regiment. Stirling was promoted to Lieutenant-Colonel. By early 1943, the establishment of the Regiment allowed for five squadrons, totalling about 600 men. From now on, the Regiment would usually find its own transport, and Special Forces activity was now so organised by Colonel Hackett that the LRDG were devoted specifically to long range work, whilst SAS raids

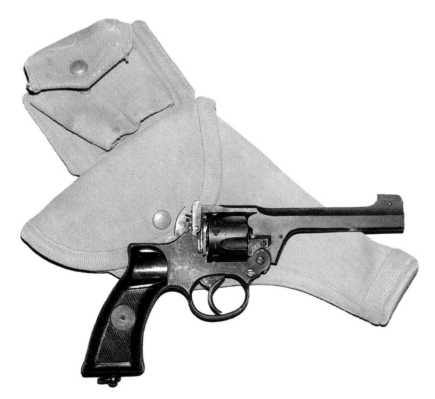

The Number 2 Mark 1,
Enfield, .38 revolver. A standard issue weapon, the six-shot Enfield revolver saw limited SAS use in the Second World War – semi-automatics seem to have been generally preferred. At least one Enfield has been found in recent years with SAS markings, though presumably this was for the guard room rather than active service, where such stampings would have compromised anonymity.**

were normally to be short distance.

On 27 January, 1943, at the pinnacle of his success, and with final Axis defeat in North Africa less than four months away, Lieutenant-Colonel Stirling was captured during a reconnaisance. The story, as related by Rommel, was as follows: 'During January, a number of our A.A. gunners succeeded in surprising a British column of the Long Range Desert Group in Tunisia and captured the commander of the 1st SAS Regiment, Lieutenant-Colonel David Stirling. Insufficiently guarded, he managed to escape and made his way to some Arabs, to whom he offered a reward if they would get him back to the British lines. But his bid must have been too small, for the Arabs, with their usual eye to business, offered him to us for 5 kg of tea – a bargain which we soon clinched. Thus the British lost the very able and adaptable commander of the desert group which had caused us more damage than any other British unit of equal strength'.

As might be expected, Stirling was not the type to take to captivity easily. First he posed as an officer of the Royal Army Service Corps, then he made numerous escape attempts, at least two before being taken away from Africa, one at Innsbruck, and another at Markt Pongau, also in Austria. Unsurprisingly he was soon categorised a high risk prisoner, and by August 1944 he was on his way to Colditz. There he shared a room with the legendary legless fighter ace Douglas Bader.

Rommel's verdict on Stirling's contribution to the desert war, and particularly on the relationship between Special Forces and the Arabs, makes interesting reading: 'These Commandos [LRDG and SAS], working from Kufra and the Qattara Depression, sometimes operated right up into Cyrenaica, where they caused considerable havoc and seriously disquieted the Italians. They tried again and again to incite the Arabs against us – fortunately with little success, for there is nothing so unpleasant as partisan warfare. It is perhaps very important not to make reprisals on hostages at the

Top, **Members of 2 SAS at Termoli, Italy, seen during an inspection by General Bernard Montgomery. Foreground, left and right, respectively are Major Sandy Scratchley DSO, MC, and Captain Roy Farran. The weapons seen include the No 4 rifle, Thompson SMG, and German MP 40. The censor has partially obliterated the cap badges. IWM E 26182**

Bottom, **2 SAS 3-inch mortar team firing in support of partisans in the Alba area of Italy. Their dress sense is characteristic: one man wears a bandanna with sweater, and a semi-automatic pistol and lanyard attached to the back of his belt; one man wears a Denison smock; the last a light-coloured waistcoat and beret.**

Previous page, Vickers machine gun team of 2 SAS parachuted in support of the partisans near Castino, Italy, 1945. For ease of carriage one man takes the tripod on his back, another the barrel, and the third takes the condenser can, whilst ammunition belts are worn around the body. Pistols and knives are carried for close combat.
IWM NA 25407

Above, Officers of 2nd SAS in conversation with partisans, Italy, 1945. The men, wearing a strange variety of both Allied and captured uniform, stand around the customized car carrying Bren guns, Sten guns, and pistols.

first outbreak of partisan warfare, for these only create feelings of revenge and serve to strengthen the *francs-tireurs*. It is better to allow an incident to go unavenged than to hit back at the innocent. It only agitates the whole neighbourhood, and hostages easily become martyrs. The Italian commander shared my view, and so the occasional Arab raid was usually overlooked.'

ACTION IN ITALY

With David Stirling in captivity and the fall of Tunis, the war moved into a new phase, and soon the SAS would be reorganised. 1st SAS commanded by Paddy Mayne was renamed Special Raiding Squadron (SRS), and prepared for immediate action against the coasts of Sicily and Italy, whilst a 2nd SAS was formed in May 1943 under David Stirling's brother Lieutenant-Colonel William Stirling, using mainly Commando personnel. The SBS achieved independence under Earl Jellicoe, and were mainly committed to Greece and the Aegean.

All parts of the Regiment were soon in action. On 28 May, 2nd SAS were involved in Operation Snapdragon reconnaisance of the island of Pantalleria. In June, during Operation Huskey, the SRS and 2nd SAS had responsibility for disrupting enemy movement on Sicily whilst the Allied invasion was underway. Similarly critical to the campaign was the destruction by the SRS of the heavy coastal battery at Capo Murro di Porco. According to Lieutenant Harrison, he was initially landed on the wrong part of the lofty rocky coast: 'Cautiously I raised my head. Where the bomb had fallen a shed was burning. In the flare of the flames I could see, only a few feet away, a tangle of wire and beyond that the menacing muzzle of a big gun. We had been advancing right into the enemy battery, and into our own mortar fire. For a moment I was tempted to rush the battery from where we were… There was only one thing to be done. Retrace our steps… From somewhere on the right

a light machine gun opened up on us as we scurried across the open ground… We were behind the battery now. Most of the buildings appeared to be blazing, and in the light of the flames we could see the guns… From behind came a sharp rattle of machine gun fire. Streams of green tracer cut through our ranks. As we dived for cover our two Bren gunners swung round firing from the hip in the direction from which the tracer had come. No more firing came from the mystery gunner… We were about to step over the one remaining wall between ourselves and the objective when, from right to our front, came a steam of red tracer. Lying full length in the nettles behind the wall – it was no more than a foot high – I yelled the challenge at the top of my voice: "Desert Rats!". Back came the answer "kill the Italians"!'

Having discovered that they had engaged their comrades in a fire fight, they now turned on the Italians who emerged from their bunkers, hands held high. The SRS were then free to move on to the next battery. At a cost of three casualties, they had taken 18 heavy guns, numerous small arms, and about 500 prisoners. Though German armour was not far away, the landing succeeded and within two days Augusta harbour was also secured. In the less dramatic Operations Chestnut and Narcissus, diversionary raids were made on the north of the island. Chestnut was widely scattered in a parachute landing, Narcissus landed from the sea but was not heavily engaged.

By September 1943, the SRS had made its presence felt on mainland Italy. On 3 September, they helped seize and hold the port of Bagnara, thus disrupting enemy communications. As on Sicily, Lieutenant Harrison was in the forefront, and as before he was landed in the wrong place. This was fortunate, since the appointed landing ground was covered by enemy positions, whilst the actual landing placed the SRS behind the German lines. Nevertheless, there was still a vicious fire fight before the raiders were able to contact British

Lieutenant Colonel 'Paddy' Blair Mayne pictured during a visit to the War Office in London. Next to David Stirling, Mayne was arguably the most famous SAS commander, having served with distinction in the earliest desert operations. Note the medal ribbons, including that for the Africa Star and insignia for 'Mention in Dispatches', SAS wings, and distinctive sand-coloured beret.

forces advancing on Bagnara from the landward side. At first the Germans were confused, taking the SRS for Italians, but then they managed to get mortars and artillery into action: 'I was showing the last man to his fire position when, from up the road, there came the sharp angry whine of a sniper's bullet. Over on the left I heard the slow, eerie whistle of mortar bombs. "Wummp – wummp – wummp – wummp". They straddled 1 Troop's positions on the lower bend. Someone shouted and a medical orderly came running up the road. Up in the hills a gun came into action. A shell whined over to fall in the town. I ducked hurriedly. The sniper was at it again.' Given the situation, the SRS were lucky to get away with relatively light casualties. Paddy Mayne distinguished himself by taking on a machine gun position with a sub-machine gun.

Though the SAS was also committed to Jeep patrols on land, the next big mission would also be from the sea. In October 1943, just over 200 men of the SRS were committed to seize the port of Termoli on the Adriatic ahead of the main Allied advance. It was more of a set piece than a raiding force might reasonably expect, and did lead to a German counter-attack. The raiders defended themselves with Brens and mortars until the Allied position was strong enough to hold. Roy Farran, who had joined the SRS by Jeep from the landward side, described it as a 'pure infantry battle'. His personal *bête noir* was a German sniper hiding in a dome overlooking the cemetery, a man who was only dislodged by fire from Sherman tanks.

Only a few days later, Operation Speedwell led by Captain Pinckney demonstrated the sort of success that Special Forces could achieve if properly used. Two seven-man patrols were parachuted into the Genoa area, and here they survived for over two months derailing trains and interfering with transport. Though one of the more productive Italian missions, Speedwell cost Pinckney his life – captured and shot by the Germans. Operations Candytuft and Saxifrage

were similarly aimed at railways, though this time the parties were landed from the sea. For the cost of two men captured, the lines were severed in 16 places, and damage inflicted on telephone and power lines. The attacks were achieved in pitch darkness and driving rain, as Roy Farran relates: 'The rain was still driving in our faces as we started the old trudge over the fields. After crawling across ditches and through hedges, we scrambled up a wet, grassy bank to the railway. We dumped our rucksacks together so that Linton could lay the charges while we guarded the area. Fumbling in the storm with the wind driving the rain up in great sprays down the line, Linton tinkered about for what seemed an age. There was a scare when a truck drove up the road. Then he stood up and said he was ready. Two minutes late, we squeezed the time delays. Picking up our packs, we rolled down the embankment to the wire fence. Before long we were fighting up muddy paths into the hills. Our flat rubber soles would not grip in the mud and often we would slide back to the bottom of the slope… After we had pulled our way by branches to the top of a particularly difficult ascent, we heard the sound of explosions and saw flashes through the rain.'

At the beginning of 1944, a series of small-scale raids were launched to hinder enemy communications and distract from the Allied landings at Anzio. These attacks included a raid on the airfield at San Egidio, and the cutting of rail links north of Rome. Some of the targets were successfully hit, but a number of SAS men were captured or missing presumed dead. Thereafter, most Special Forces personnel were withdrawn for the invasion of France, although 2nd SAS would again be active in Italy in 1945.

The most important of these actions during the closing months of the war were Operations Tombola, Galia, and Cold Comfort. Galia was a co-operation with partisans to aid the advance of the US Army. Cold Comfort was an imaginative, but ultimately disastrous, attempt to block the

Opposite, **SAS men with a Jeep during Operation Bulbasket, behind enemy lines, France, June 1944. Apart from the Vickers K, several pistols and a Sten gun are in evidence.** *IWM HU 66220*

Brenner Pass. In Tombola, Major Farran, Captain Jock Eyston, and Lieutenant Ken Harvey with 50 men of 3 Squadron lent support to the partisan campaign in the vicinity of Albinea. The force was organised into a three-company Alleato Battalion in which the SAS was one company, and the other two were made up of escaped Russian prisoners, *Wehrmacht* deserters of the 162nd Turkoman Division, and Italians.

Uniform was distinctly optional in the Alleato, being a mixture of British, American, German, and Italian — the Italians favouring neckerchiefs of parachute silk of various hues. Numbers had to be made up with what Farran described as 'long-haired youths', but equipment was tolerably good, including a three-inch mortar, bazookas, Bren guns, Thompson sub-machine guns, various rifles, and pistols. The officers found horses to ride, and music was provided by a piper of the Highland Light Infantry complete with kilt. Intelligence was gathered by a 15-strong squad of Italian girls on bicycles. A German diesel lorry was captured by means of a man standing in the road in German uniform who shot the driver as soon as he stopped. This served as transport, but eventually had to be towed by bullocks. Reviewing the outfit, Farran was stuck by its resemblance to 'a tableau of Wat Tyler's rebellion'.

Members of 1 SAS Regiment pictured in June 1944 with their camouflaged Jeep in Le Fôret de Verrieres, near Chateauroux, France, during Operation Bulbasket. The soldier foreground right wears sweater, pistol belt, and Airborne Forces battle dress trousers with expanding map pocket. All these men, except Johnnie Holmes, seated foreground left, were captured and executed by the Germans in July 1944.

Despite their curious appearance and losses in action, the Alleato did good service, wrecking German 51 Corps Headquarters, and killing a German general under cover of darkness. Lieutenant Harvey was particularly conspicuous in his gallantry: 'At Villa Calvi Ken Harvey killed two sentries on the lawn before they realised they were being attacked. The front door was locked, but was soon burst with a bazooka bomb. Four Germans were killed on the ground floor, but others fought back valiantly down the spiral staircase. In one room, Harvey was confronted by a German with a Schmeisser. He ducked but neglected to extinguish his torch. Fortunately Sergeant Godwin was quick with his tommy gun, and shot over Harvey's shoulder. Several attempts were made to get up the stairs, but the Germans kept up a concentrated fire… Corporal Leyburn was wounded with a grenade rolled down from above. Another British parachutist called Mulvey was hit in the knee with a bullet.

'From the lawn outside an equally furious battle raged against the top windows. Several Germans were killed by bazooka and tommy gun fire. Harvey realised that it was impossible to take the house in the 20 minutes allowed. He therefore decided to start a fire on the ground floor. Working frantically against time, the British heaped up maps, chairs, files and curtains in a great pyre in the middle of the operations room. With the aid of a few pounds of explosive and a bottle of petrol, the trail was laid and ignited.'

INTO FRANCE

In the spring of 1944, the Special Raiding Squadron and 2nd SAS returned from Italy, and were reorganised together with 3rd and 4th French SAS, a Belgian Squadron, and F Phantom Squadron to create a formidable concentration of Special Forces in the SAS Brigade. The brigade was commanded by Brigadier R.W. McLeod, and formed a part of Lieutenant General Frederick

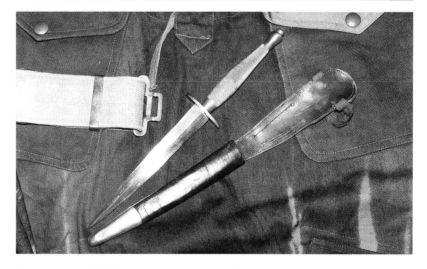

Top, Detail of the US M1 Carbine, as carried by the SAS in the latter part of the Second World War. A semi-automatic weapon weighing just 5 lb, the M1 was an ideal back-up to machine guns; its only real drawback was short effective range.

Middle, Detail of the bolt action .303 inch, Number 4 Rifle. Standard British Army issue. The Number 4 saw use with the Regiment from the middle of the Second World War. Fitted with a telescopic sight, it made a useful sniper weapon.

Bottom, The Fairbairn Sykes fighting knife and 1937 Pattern webbing belt, seen against the Denison parachute smock. The 'FS' knife, or 'Commando Dagger', was invented by Captains W.E. Fairbairn and E.A. Sykes of the Shanghai Police, who later served the Army as unarmed and close quarter combat instructors. The first order for official purposes was made to Wilkinson Sword early in 1941. Though used by the SAS, it thus predates the formation of the Regiment.

Browning's 1st Airborne Corps. As part of an Airborne Forces formation, the SAS now adopted the red beret of the paratrooper, though strictly speaking this headgear was more maroon or claret in colour, the actual shade having been selected by Sir Alan Brooke, with, it is said, the assistance of Browning's wife, Daphne du Maurier, in 1942. The Brigade now underwent a period of intensive training in Scotland. Lieutenant Harrison recalled three months of day and night marches over the Scottish hills, 'our rucksacks weighted with filled sandbags', and small charges to be laid on dummy targets. Groups practised the cutting of telephone wires, attacking stations, and entering submarine facilities, often using Home Guards as practice opposition. Lectures were given on the rudiments of undercover work, escape, and evasion. One lecturer was said to have advised his students that the best way to contact potentially friendly French civilians was after dark on their way to an outside lavatory, a lesson which caused some merriment. Parachuting skills were also learned, or re-learned with the use of suspended drop bags: 'These leg-bags were roughly the same shape and size as an ordinary army kit bag, and were used to carry the equipment we dropped with. Secured to the right leg with two straps, a pull on the quick release cord freed it immediately, allowing it to swing from the belt at the end of a 20 foot length of rope. Although heavy and cumbersome in the extreme, it avoided the danger of having to run the gauntlet of enemy fire while dashing to and fro undoing supply containers dropped separately. Hanging there 20 feet below, the leg-bag had the added advantage of "feeling the ground" on a night drop. As the bag touched down, the chute, released from the extra weight, billowed and "breathed", giving a lighter landing and warning of its imminence'.

Just how the Regiment should contribute to the assault on western Europe was a vexed question. One plan put forward was that the SAS Brigade

Lieutenant Dain and Captain J. Tonkin of 1st SAS pictured near Lesignac during Operation Bulbasket, 1944. Dain, with two semi-automatic pistols pushed into his waist band, wears the Airborne Forces version of the battle dress trousers with the map pocket on his left thigh. Tonkin's extraordinary armament is a 9 mm *Luger Lange Pistole* of the type used by German artillerymen in the First World War.

would be dropped immediately behind the German front line. Here they would ambush enemy reinforcements and sever communication with the battle front, helping conventional forces to win the campaign. This was seen by many as a misuse of the SAS, committing them tactically to a pitched engagement which would squander a strategic resource. Bill Stirling, commander of 2nd SAS resigned over this point and was replaced by Lieutenant Colonel Brian Franks. In the end it was decided that the SAS role would be threefold: arming and training the French Resistance in interfering with enemy reinforcement; raiding in vehicles; and locating railway targets for either

RAF or SAS attack. The result was a multitude of insertions behind enemy lines, some of which reaped remarkable rewards.

First actions were to commence the night before D-Day. In Operation Titanic IV, two three-man patrols were planned to be dropped inland of the Normandy beaches with instructions to make as much noise and confusion as possible, laying ambushes on roads, and thereby misleading the Germans as to the real parachute landing grounds. SAS efforts were to be supported by the dropping of one-third-scale dummy parachutists, 'rifle simulator' fire crackers, and 'pintail' bombs which let off Verey light cartridges. The subterfuge was

Captain Tonkin, left, with Lieutenants Stephens and Crisp 1st SAS, France 1944. Lieutenant Stephens shows a French style disguise. The other officers have pistols with lanyards.
IWM HU 66212

further aided by loading the SAS aircraft with empty weapons containers and packing materials to be strewn around to suggest the site of supply drops. In the event, Lieutenant N.H. Poole, the mission commander, tripped over his drop bag exiting the air craft and was knocked unconscious, whilst the other officer landed wide, and some of the equipment was lost. Nevertheless Troopers Dawson, Saunders, Hurst and Merryweather carried on with the assignment, exploding 20 Lewis bombs before melting into the countryside to join the Resistance. All six men were at liberty for about a month before being captured.

The same night, Operations Samwest and Dingson dropped about 30 French SAS men and a guide in Brittany to set up bases, from which they would harry the enemy in concert with the Resistance. A fire fight resulted in some losses, but the French SAS presence was built up by further drops, until over 400 men were acting in co-operation with a greater number of the *Maquis*. On 12 June, the Germans attacked the covert parties at the Samwest base area in the Fôret de Duault, alerted it is said by the French SAS men's propensity for eating in local restaurants. The enemy deployed 13 truckloads of troops supported by flame-throwers, which were used to burn the forest. In the ensuing defensive battles, casualties were suffered on both sides, though the SAS base near Vannes survived to fight again, aided by the local Special Operations Executive (SOE) Jedburgh team. Guerrilla fighting continued despite savage reprisals visited on the local population by *Ostbataillon* Russian troops employed by the Germans, and the French SAS were still in action when US Third Army finally liberated Brittany. The whole episode provided valuable experience but also underlined the fact that the *Maquis* could be a double-edged sword. They were often the terror of the enemy, and could provide a useful element of surprise, but were by no means the same as regular troops. Perhaps the bleakest

estimate of *Maquis* value was provided by Lieutenant Riding of the SAS: 'Their main desire seemed to be to get arms and hold the local farmers (or anyone else against whom they held a grudge) to ransom. They had no discipline or organisation and went to pieces when attacked'.

Of all the SAS operations mounted in conjunction with the Normandy campaign, it was Operation Bulbasket which had the most difficult job, and had most at stake. Bulbasket began the night before D-Day when two officers of B Squadron 1st SAS were dropped in the Vienne area, well inland, to begin activities against rail targets. One of these officers, Captain John Tonkin, was to command the operation. Soon the group was built up to a total of 43 men of B Squadron, and 12 from Phantom Squadron. They promptly achieved a major *coup* when they received intelligence of a rail spur in the woods near Châtelleraut, on which the Germans had hidden 11 tankers of fuel intended for the *SS Panzer Division Das Reich*, then on its way to Normandy. RAF and Commonwealth ground attack was called in, and Mosquito fighter bombers turned the depot into an inferno. The rail line to Tours was also cut repeatedly, and a train derailed. Bulbasket made a significant contribution to the Normandy invasion, helping, in concert with air attack, to slow and hamper a major German armoured formation.

The Bulbasket team received Jeeps, and set up a base near Verriers, but were compromised. According to one account, the SAS were discovered when two French collaborators, posing as *Maquis*, came to the area under pretence of getting repairs to a motorcycle. The attack led by *Oberleutnant* Vogt came at dawn on 3 July, when few of the defenders were alert. The Germans were evidently well prepared, hammering the position with mortars and machine guns before closing in. In all, 31 of the Bulbasket team were captured or killed. The prisoners were ruthlessly exterminated. Tonkin was lucky to make his escape, and together with other survivors was flown out

Opposite, **Sergeant Goffinet, 5th Belgian SAS (1st Belgian Independent Parachute Squadron) is presented with the Military Medal by Major General Surtees in the Grand Place, Brussels, 20 October 1945. Note the British-type battle dress, and the Pegasus arm insignia with SAS wings above.**

from a makeshift strip from behind enemy lines.

Operation Gain led by Ian Fenwick, commander of D Squadron, also succeeded in some disruption of rail traffic in the Fontainebleau area south-west of Paris. Yet Gain seems to have come under pressure almost from the start, perhaps because it was based near a large centre of population, and had to move its location several times. At night, activities were continually interrupted by enemy vehicles, and the SAS took to driving around with their headlights on in the hope that they might be mistaken for Germans. By bluff and daring, Fenwick was able to mount an attack on the engine sheds near Fontainebleau, and ambushes on the Orleans to Pithiviers road. Finally the tables were turned and the Germans began to attempt to ambush the SAS as they traversed the countryside. Fenwick was killed when he tried to take on one of these enemy ambush parties. Only one man in Fenwick's Jeep would live, Corporal Duffy, who eventually escaped from a hospital disguised as a German medical officer. Gain also suffered a serious setback when a dozen parachute reinforcements under Captain Garstin were compromised and killed or captured. The prisoners were to be executed a little while later, though this was bungled, with the result that Corporals Jones and Vaculik escaped to tell the tale.

Operation Gaff also had problems, but for different reasons. Gaff's objective was the killing or capture of Field Marshal Rommel, whose headquarters had been identified at La Roche Guyon on the Seine. Captain William Lee and six men were duly parachuted in on 25 July, but before they could launch an assault, Rommel was wounded by RAF ground attack. Captain Lee devoted his energies to attacking trains and a raid on the enemy headquarters at Mantes, until the US Army overran the area.

Though there were many operations, it was Houndsworth which made the most sustained SAS contribution in the wake of D-Day. Houndsworth would eventually see the whole of A Squadron, 1st SAS, under Major Fraser operating in the Fôret du Morvan south-west of Dijon. Here they conducted a three-month campaign, including the various Toby missions, which involved appearing and disappearing from the woods to disrupt the Paris, Dijon, and Lyon rail routes. By the end of June, the A Squadron battle-group would have at its disposal 144 men, nine Jeeps, two six pounder anti-tank guns, and numerous machine guns and mortars. Dropping Jeeps by parachute and freeing them if they landed off the drop zone in woodland was an art in itself, but in this, as in many other tasks the SAS were aided by the Resistance.

Once retrieved, there was more work to do on the heavily armed transport, as Lieutenant Harrison related of a later drop: 'The new Jeeps had to be fitted up. The first thing to do was to allocate crews to the Jeeps – driver, commander (who was front gunner), and rear gunner. As soon as this was done, the crews set to work on the vehicles. Auxiliary petrol tanks had been fitted, one under the commander's seat and two over the lockers in the back, giving each Jeep a capacity of 48 gallons and a road range of some 900 miles at one filling. But the feed pipes had to be connected.

'The guns, too, had been parachuted separately. Mountings had to be assembled and guns aligned. These mountings, made from tubular steel, were of a heavier type than those used in the desert and, we were to find out later, much less satisfactory. The guns, mounted in pairs, were the Vickers K gas-operated aircraft guns, with a rate of fire of around 1,200 a minute. The 100-round magazines were loaded up with tracer, armour piercing and incendiary bullets. One or two magazines were loaded up exclusively with ball, or ordinary bullets. These were for use when it was particularly important not to give away our position to the enemy… Apart from the twin Vickers front and rear, there was a single Vickers mounted by the driver which could be fired while he drove one-handed. Carried loose in the back for dismounted action was a Bren gun. Hand grenades were tucked away in various odd spots all over the Jeep. They were ideal for breaking off an engagement… pins withdrawn, and dropped over the back of the withdrawing Jeep, they worked wonders.' Finally, close by each member of the crew, easily accessible, were his carbine and escape haversack.' Later, when Allied ground support aircraft dominated the sky over the A Squadron bases, the Jeeps took to flying Union Jacks in an attempt to avoid strafing by friendly fire.

In many instances, especially when rail lines or intelligence were the objective, SAS patrols avoided contacts, or moved under cover of darkness. At other times fire fights were unavoidable. On one occasion the Houndsworth SAS came to the assistance of the *Maquis*, driving off an enemy incursion with an anti-tank gun . On another, they attacked a convoy transporting deportees, allowing the prisoners to escape. One night in August, Alec Muirhead took the 3-inch mortar crews within range of the synthetic fuel plant at Autun, and set light to it with a bombardment of high explosive and phosphorous bombs. The defenders retired to shelter, believing they were under air attack. Eventually, Houndsworth teams ranged over a total area of almost 6,000 square miles, broke rail lines on no less than 22 occasions, reported 30 targets to the RAF, and killed, wounded, or captured approximately 300 Germans. The 3rd French SAS achieved a similar level of success in the Nantes and Samur areas of western France during Operation Dickens, where the rail network eventually ground to a complete halt. The destruction of 200 enemy vehicles was claimed.

TO THE RHINE AND BEYOND

With the Allied break-out from Normandy in mid-August 1944, the war moved into a new phase. For the SAS, this would mean more even more aggressive operations along the potential lines of advance, disrupting enemy communications and spreading havoc in the rear areas. One of the first actions of the break-out was Operation Trueform, which saw 102 men of 1st, 2nd, and Belgian SAS dropped on 12 landing zones north-west of Paris on 17 August. Trueform achieved some destruction of enemy vehicles and supplies, but was overtaken by the headlong Allied advance in little more than a week. At Saone, French 3rd SAS provided support for the right flank of Patton's 3rd US Army, destroying bridges and railways, and laying mines during Operation Harrod. Later, French 4th SAS were similarly employed on an even larger mission, Operation Spenser, which harassed the enemy as they retreated across the Loire.

Operation Kipling was one of the most important of the break-out phase, initiated on 13 August 1944, with a view to preparing for a major Allied airborne landing around the Orleans gap. So it was that C Squadron 1st SAS built up a presence of 107 men in a series of drops near Toucy, not far from Auxerre in central France. Their initial remit was intelligence and liaison, but with the cancellation of the main parachute drop, Kipling was ordered onto the offensive, a role which C Squadron adopted with gusto. One SAS Jeep drove into a German cycle patrol and sprayed them with machine gun fire as they tried to make their escape. According to one account, eight prisoners from this encounter were later executed by the *Maquis*. Another prisoner, taken in a road ambush willingly became a cook and handyman for the SAS, rather than risk being given to the Resistance.

Once Allied ground troops were in the vicinity, the Jeep patrols of Kipling became even bolder, but this bravado almost cost Lieutenant Harrison his life when he drove into the enemy-occupied village of Les Ormes: 'I took in the scene in an instant. The church in the middle of the square… a large truck… two German staff cars… the crowd of *SS* men in front of the church… The staff cars and the

Next page, SAS patrol in Malaya. Interesting details include the rucksacks, jungle boots, and US-made .30 calibre M1 Carbines.

truck burst into flames as, standing in my seat, I raked the square with fire from my twin machine guns. The crowds of *SS* men stampeded for cover. Many of them died in those few seconds in front of the church, lit by the flickering flames of the burning vehicles.

'Even as I fired I shouted to Hall to reverse. The Jeep jerked to a halt about 30 yards from the church. The Germans who had escaped the first fury of our assault were now returning our fire. I turned to see why Hall had not got the Jeep moving back. He lay slumped over the wheel. The tell-tale gouts of blood told their own story. Curly Hall was dead.

'Still firing I pressed the starter with my foot. The engine was still, hit by the burst of fire that got Hall. Then my guns jammed. No time to try to put them right. I dashed round to use the rear gun. It fired one burst, and stopped. There was now only the single gun by the driver's seat. I got round to it and managed to fire a couple of short bursts…'

Outflanked by enemy infantry advancing through an orchard, Harrison was reduced to engaging them with his M1 carbine, before being hit in the hand and making a desperate dash for other vehicles in his group. With a finger already broken on the other hand, Harrison found himself next to useless and was extremely lucky to survive a bumpy, hell-for-leather, escape in a comrade's Jeep along a woodland ride. It was some consolation to discover that his patrol had in fact interrupted a mass execution of villagers at Les Ormes, many of whom had succeeded in making off when the SAS appeared on the scene.

One of the most successful exploitation exercises of this period was Operation Wallace, the 2nd SAS dash across France led by Major Roy Farran, which was designed to link up with the base of Operation Hardy on the Plateau de Langres near Châtillon. The technique was simple, though often fraught with danger. Since the front was now in a state of flux, Farran and his team of 60 men in

Sergeant Hannah, SAS, after a successful jump into the forest, Malaya.

20 Jeeps was landed at Rennes Airfield on 19 August, and driven past strong points through the retreating Germans. The Jeep column was broken down into three groups which moved at half hour intervals, bypassing the opposition. Each group would attempt to warn the others of the enemy locations by radio. For 50 miles, Farran make excellent progress, until the inevitable happened: 'We turned a corner to come face to face with a 75 mm gun blocking the entire road. Even as I told Corporal Clarke, my driver, to swing into the ditch, two Germans in *Afrika Korps* hats fired a shell at less than 10 yards' range. Perhaps it was because we were so close to the muzzle of the gun that the shell whistled over our heads to burst in the road behind.

'And then we were crawling out of the wrecked Jeep into the ditch with bullets spattering all round. The little *Maquis* guide… was shot in the knee. As I huddled under the bank, I could see the spare wheel from the front of the Jeep rolling down the middle of the road. There were lots of Germans practically on top of us, shouting wildly and spraying the Jeep with machine gun fire. We crawled about five yards from the vehicle when I remembered the codes and my marked map. Carpendale, the Signals Officer, crawled back to get them. We still had the Bren, so that when we came to a convenient gully I sent the others to the top of the bank to hold them off. I began to run the gauntlet back to organise the rest of the column.' The remaining Jeeps which had halted round the corner, believing Farran to have hit a mine, were now directed either side, wide of the obstructed lane, in an attempt to outflank the enemy:

'By now the enemy fire had become very heavy, including shells and mortar bombs. The Germans made a foolish charge along both sides of the road, giving us a magnificent shot at less than 50 yards' range. Their casualties were very heavy and Jim Mackie's troop alone accounted for a whole platoon in a field. Instead of abandoning the attack,

the idiots came on until they were so far into our rough semi-circle that we were cutting them down on three sides. I even shot a German with my own carbine – my only definite personal bag of the war.'

Despite the damage inflicted, the SAS were well advised to break off what was fast becoming a full-scale action, in which their radio trailer was destroyed. Similar encounter battles would account for 13 of Operation Wallace's vehicles, though a number of men who were assumed dead made their way back to Allied lines. The remainder of Farran's column were lucky enough to intercept a large German goods train, which they sprayed with armour-piercing bullets, wrecking it and killing its guards. They saw off the defenders of a radar station, before they finally relieved Grant-Hibberd's Hardy base camp. The two SAS groups then worked in concert. In a month behind enemy lines, the mission had claimed many enemy casualties, a train, 95 vehicles, and a vital 100,000 gallons of petrol – for the loss of 16 SAS men. Grant-Hibberd's party had severed the Dijon rail line, attacked a post on the main road, and interfered with power supply by blowing up pylons.

Much less successful was Operation Leyton in the Vosges, where 91 men of 2 SAS and Phantom under Lieutenant Colonel Franks attempted to gather intelligence and open the way for American

Welcome respite for men of the Regiment in Malaya. Though progressively longer periods were spent in the jungle, a long campaign meant there were still sessions of training elsewhere. These enabled new techniques to be assimilated.

armour. Here the SAS were up against not only anti-partisan units from Nancy and Strasbourg, but very unreliable *Maquis* assistance. The project was only intended to run for a week or two, but the pace of the Allied advance had slowed, and by October there was still no sign of relief. To make matters worse, the Germans started deporting the populations of villages which offered help, and many civilians were shot. Since they were doing little good and in constant danger of compromise, Franks decided that his party should extricate itself. This was easier said than done: part of the SAS party was overrun by enemy armour, a couple killed in action, and a number executed out of hand. In all, about a third of the Leyton team perished.

Though the Belgian SAS (also known as the Belgian Independent Parachute Company or 5th SAS) had been usefully employed in France, it was in late August and September 1944 that they really came into their own, being dropped into their own country and the French Ardennes, as the advance guard of the Allied assault. One of their most extraordinary missions was Operation Fabian, across the border in the Netherlands, during which the Belgian SAS was intended to gather information on the V2 rocket sites. The mission commenced in mid-September 1944, but was rudely interrupted by Market Garden and the Arnhem debacle. The leader of the mission, Lieutenant G.S. Kirschen, then turned his talents to aiding the escaping British paratroops, during which time he lived in a hen house. Operation Fabian was only finally wound up in March 1945.

In the autumn of 1944, the war in the west was on the borders of the *Reich*, and from then on few opportunities would present themselves for truly strategic behind-the-lines activities. One of the last classic infiltrations was Operation Pistol in which 51 men of 2nd SAS were dropped in Alsace-Lorraine on 15 September. Pistol knocked out four enemy trains, some vehicles, and a rail line between the Rhine and Moselle, but it also resulted in some of the team being captured before the arrival of American troops in early October.

According to Otway's *Airborne Forces*, by November 1944 the SAS had an impressive tally of destruction to their credit in north-west Europe. This included over 700 enemy road vehicles, 29 locomotives, 89 rail trucks, and several thousand enemy personnel accounted casualties or prisoners. Perhaps even more importantly, about 400 targets had been reported to the RAF for air attack. Yet this was not without cost: 300 SAS men were lost, and the RAF had flown 780 sorties, dropping over 10,000 containers and panniers, both to insert and supply the Special Forces campaign. In doing so they had lost six aircraft. Material considerations were not therefore entirely one-sided, yet there was undoubtedly a strategic dimension to this SAS effort. German movements had been hampered at significant points, enemy personnel had been tied down on often fruitless defensive duties, and occupied populations had been given concrete evidence of Allied intent often by their own countrymen in SAS uniform.

Wisely, relatively few Special Forces actions were attempted inside Germany, where hostile populations might have led to unacceptable losses. Nevertheless, the SAS continued to make itself useful in a reconnaissance role. Mayne's 1st SAS

SAS man with captured Communist 'bandit', Malaya. The SAS man's 'uniform' comprises a pair of light-weight trousers and a sweat band around the head.

operated with the Canadian 4th Armoured Division in the difficult country of Holland, and it was also here, in Operations Keystone, Larkswood, and Amherst, that valuable work was done by 2nd, French, and Belgian SAS preventing the destruction of bridges and assisting the Resistance. Remarkably, Mayne won his fourth Distinguished Service Order on 9 April 1945 as the Canadians pushed into Oldenburg. Ambushed by a German *Panzerfaust* team, Mayne picked up a Bren gun and launched a daring rescue of his trapped colleagues. Not long after, Mayne drove over an enemy machine gun emplacement, then calmly alighted to fire into the position from the rear. Surprisingly, he was not killed.

The final SAS operation in the west was Archway, in which Squadrons from 1st and 2nd SAS crossed the Rhine in support of 21st Army Group. They reached the port of Kiel on 3 May 1945. By now, Brigadier McLeod had been given a staff job in India, and for the closing stages of the war command of SAS Brigade had gone to Brigadier Mike Calvert. So it was that when 1st and 2nd SAS were moved to Bergen in Norway for the disarming of the enemy garrison at the end of hostilities, the Brigade was led by Brigadier Mike Calvert.

With the sudden collapse of Japan in August 1945, the SAS found itself without a role. In September, the Belgian SAS Regiment was formally handed over to the control of its own national government. The French followed suit the next month. On 8 October 1945, the 1st and 2nd SAS were paraded for the last time and disbanded. This, however, was not quite the end, since the Chief of the Imperial General Staff did order a report to be produced with recommendations for the use of the SAS in 'the next war', and for the best composition of the Regiment in such an eventuality.

Mike Calvert grasped this slender straw enthusiastically, offering the opinion that the SAS had proved itself adaptable to any theatre, strategically useful in defensive as well as offensive campaigns, relatively inexpensive, and better than 'private armies'. Having canvassed other SAS and Special Forces officers like David Stirling, Earl Jellicoe, Paddy Mayne and Roy Farran, Calvert reported that the Regiment would be more important in the next war than the last. New wars might not have static front lines, and a force of disciplined troops operating in the enemy rear would be invaluable. It was decided that when the Territorial Army was recreated in 1947, its order of battle should include an SAS regiment.

This new part-time formation would be led by Lieutenant Colonel Brian Franks, former commanding officer of 2nd SAS, and at least some of its men were veterans of former campaigns. The unit would be based at Euston, London, and its title would be 21st Special Air Service Regiment (Artists Rifles). It is said that the number '21' was a reversal of the old regimental numbers 1st and 2nd. The Artists Rifles title was a survival from the old 38th Middlesex (Artists) Rifle Volunteer Corps, which had originally been raised in 1860 at the Arts Club on Hanover Square, London, as just one of many part-time volunteer units formed to face the threat of French invasion. Traditionally, the Artists had been literally that, recruiting artists and other individualists to the volunteers. After various re-numberings and reorganisations, the old Artists had emerged as 28th (County of London) Battalion Artists Rifles. In 1914, the Artists had formed three battalions (later reduced to two), and one of these had gone to France. They soon established a role as officer training units, and in the Great War provided over 10,000 officers to the army. Perhaps the most tangible assets that the old Artists passed on after the Second World War were a drill hall in Duke's Road, and the classical looking Mars and Minerva cap badge, to be worn on the parachutists' red beret whilst the SAS badge was moved to the arm. Mars and Minerva was also adopted as the title of the regimental journal. According to an official

SAS publication, *The Artists and the SAS*, the Territorials were actually prepared to go to Suez in 1956 but this never actually happened.

SAS IN MALAYA

For some, the Second World War had no conclusive ending. In Malaya, which had been occupied by the Japanese, there were factions for whom Allied victory was not the result they were seeking. The Malayan Communist Party had been founded in 1930 and was naturally opposed to the British administration, but any thought of insurrection had been put on hold by the Japanese intervention and the role of Soviet Russia on the side of the Allied powers. Many Communists had fought the Japanese, and a British unit, 101 Special Training School, was formed to help the Chinese in Malaya, whilst Force 136 had been created to co-ordinate activity in occupied countries from Ceylon. One member of Force 136 was Major C.E. (Dare) Newell, Adjutant of the SAS, who was actually parachuted into Malaya towards the end of the war. By 1945, there was a covert 7,000-man Malayan People's Anti-Japanese Army in existence, supported by many sympathisers known as *Min Yuen*. The contribution of this guerrilla army to Allied victory was acknowledged by Britain with the award of an OBE to its leader, Chin Peng. Yet with

The moon-like landscape of the Jebel Akhdar, Oman.

the war over, and British prestige dented, former Allies began to fall out. The beginning of success for Mao in China and the British retreat from India seemed to suggest that the time of the Malayan Communists had come.

The year 1948 marked the opening of a campaign of terror against British rule. Rubber planters were murdered and in June a State of Emergency was declared. For 18 months the authorities grappled clumsily with an enemy who struck at soft targets then melted into the jungle. Though they succeeded in killing many terrorists, regular British battalions proved less than adept at following the enemy into their jungle lairs, or separating them from their civilian supporters. An early experiment saw the formation of a body known as Ferret Force, using volunteers, veterans of the old Force 136, and skilled Dyak trackers imported from Borneo. This exercise was promising, as Ferret Force managed to discover a number of guerrilla camps, but the killing continued as the enemy managed to slip away and sustain their campaign.

By 1950, it was clear that the British needed a new strategy, not only to protect targets and combat the terrorists, but to deny them support and the cover of the jungle. This was the genesis of the Briggs Plan, evolved by Director of Operations Sir Harold Briggs. The analysis put forward by Briggs was relatively simple. The *Min Yuen* were difficult to deal with because they were essentially civilian, organised into secret cells, and afraid of terrorist reprisals if they failed to aid the Communists. To deal with the *Min Yuen*, Briggs proposed to resettle the squatter populations in protected villages. Here the people would be given a sufficiently good standard of living that they would have no incentive to return to their impoverished camps or to provide active support to the Communists.

The Briggs Plan was further reinforced by the Emergency Powers Act, which provided both carrot and stick in dealing with the terrorist menace, including a sliding scale of cash payments which could be made to locals in return for their help. For information, $50 to $100 was paid; for the capture or killing of any terrorist, $2,000 or more was the blood money. At the same time, any who surrendered voluntarily were assured of good treatment, provided only that they were not found guilty of murder. A number of those who gave themselves up were turned, becoming guides for the security forces. Regulations also permitted detention without trial, and the potentially embarrassing problem of civilians who remained sympathetic to the Communists was removed by the deportation of over 14,000 people to mainland China. Creating defended villages, moving the population, and administering the new system could be handled by the police and regular troops.

The culmination of the Briggs plan was to clear the enemy from their jungle lairs. This was where Mike Calvert came in, and even prior to Briggs' appointment, Calvert was giving thought to the matter. After studying the problem, he suggested the raising of a Special Force, more cohesive than Ferret Force, and specifically intended to winkle out the elusive enemy. The force would be called the Malayan Scouts (SAS), and recruiting commenced immediately. Getting men proved more difficult than Calvert might have imagined, for though he naturally tried to recruit SAS veterans, there were nothing like enough for the plan in hand. He therefore had to be less discerning than he would have liked, and numbers were made up from some very odd sources. One account has it that he even accepted 10 men who were deserters from the French Foreign Legion. Not all the officers had Special Forces or jungle fighting experience either. Captain Patrick Winter recalled that he was given a few questions in a 'Chinese coffee shop' and admitted by Calvert mainly on the strength of his Scots Guards background. Calvert, however, was lucky in his choice of second in command,

in that he was able to obtain Major John Harrington, a Military Cross winner who had served with him in the Chindits.

The manpower problem was ultimately solved in several different ways. A draft was obtained from 21 SAS, the Territorial SAS unit then based in London. These arrived as M Independent Squadron, but were soon re-christened B Squadron. It took some time for the various elements to learn to respect each other and work together. A Squadron, who were predominantly veterans, mixed with the odds and ends that Calvert had managed to scrounge, soon acquired a reputation for scruffiness and hard drinking. B Squadron fancied themselves proper soldiers and were good raw material, but as yet had precious little idea about the jungle. As Sergeant Major Bob Bennett recalled: 'We became B Squadron and our first couple of training operations were a bit of a farce. On the first one we were sent off to "stonk" a grid

A Christmas Day briefing for the SAS in 1958, a few weeks prior to the attack on the Jebel Akhdar, Oman.
SAS Association

Top, SAS on the Jebel Akhdar after the attack on Suleiman's cave, indicated top right of the picture.
Middle, Peter de la Billière, left, and Johnny Watts commander of D Squadron on the ridge overlooking Habib, Jebel Akhdar, December 1958.
Bottom, One of the unreliable mules, loaded up for a climb into the mountains.

reference with 3-inch mortars and water-cooled Vickers, would you believe. God knows what was supposed to be there. I'm glad it wasn't me but we were getting a bit disillusioned then. The second consisted of us being sent off to a swampy area for eight days or so and being told to make ourselves familiar with it. It was a pretty grotty area, as swamps are, and when we came out Calvert asked me what I thought. I said we'd seen nothing and it was a bit of a waste of time. He laughed and said that's what he thought but it was good training anyway.'

In September 1950, Rhodesia agreed to provide a token force of volunteers to support the British effort in Malaya. So it was that an extra 100 officers and men under Captain Peter Walls were recruited. Arriving in Singapore in March 1951, this body was fitted into Calvert's existing structure as C Squadron (Rhodesia) Malayan Scouts (SAS). On the face of it, the least promising unit was the last to be formed. This was D Squadron, made up of volunteers fresh from the Airborne Forces Depot at Aldershot.

BOOBY TRAPS

Actual operations began in late 1950, with Operations Prosaic, Sunset, and Warbler executed during 1951. As John Woodhouse, commanding B Squadron recalled, it was stealth and booby traps which were initial mainstays of operational tactics: 'I picked a starting point, a few miles north of Chaah, for the squadron to enter the area. There we would cut a DZ [Drop Zone] and make a base. I would take a supply drop on the DZ sufficient to last the squadron for a month. Once this was done three out of my four troops would move out to far corners of our area to search for the enemy… Good tracks which radiated from Squadron HQ were carefully concealed so that they would not be spotted from existing tracks which may be used by the enemy.

'My main weapon against the Communist terrorists was to be the booby trap. It had not been used before in Johore, and I intended to use it on the largest possible scale. I had been told… that the Communist terrorists often returned to their old camps, so I ordered any camp I found unoccupied to be booby trapped. I also decided to close all main tracks we found by putting trip wires across them attached to eight grenades. In the camps, we would bury mortar bombs, connecting them to small pressure switches which would detonate them if trodden on. Great care would have to be taken to avoid leaving any sign that we had visited the camps. Booby traps were to be inspected – from a safe distance – once in every 10 to 20 days. However, in most cases I hoped that the explosion

of one would be heard by the Troop in the area. In that case they would rush to the scene.'

In case of contacts, the reserve Troop which was kept back at squadron HQ was also called upon to reinforce the patrolling Troops. In such instances, perhaps only five men were left in the jungle HQ, and every precaution was needed against enemy attack. Timber and earth would be collected to protect sentry posts, booby traps with stakes, grenades, and trip wires would be laid on approaches, a flame thrower was obtained for close defence, and a codeword was pre-planned for calling in an air strike on the position. The booby traps achieved some success before resulting in

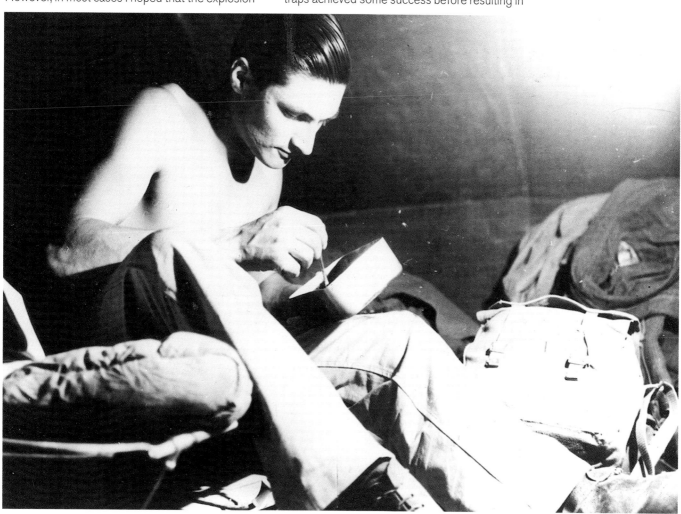

Sergeant Medic Bill Evans makes short work of the contents of his mess tin. Evans was known as the fastest eater in the regiment – the ability to eat and sleep anywhere are regimental virtues.

The Sterling 9mm SMG
seen in the hands of a
soldier of an unidentified
unit in the Gulf. The Sterling
saw extensive service with
the regiment in the 1950s
and 1960s. It was robust
and reliable, performing well
even in sand and cold, and
was fed from a side-mounted
34-round magazine.

the injury of a couple of SAS men. The result was that an embargo was placed on their use.

There were also lessons learned concerning equipment, as one NCO would relate: 'We wore green cotton shirts and trousers which were generally OK, though they would start to chafe you when you were wet, and you'd be wearing them for a week or so, but we also had these terrible boots which, believe it or not , had been specially designed by some boffin for use in the jungle. They were made of green canvas with a rubber sole and they laced up to just below your knees, and they had little eyelets which were meant to help ventilate your feet and let the water out. In fact what happened was that these little holes let sand and grit in… which caused blisters… and the canvas and rubber started to fall apart after a week or so.'

The Regiment was growing in experience, but 1951 also marked the nadir of British fortunes with the killing of Sir Henry Gurney, the High Commissioner. His replacement, General Gerald, later Field Marshal Templer, would combine the office of High Commissioner with that of Director of Operations, and quickly exhibited a determination to prosecute what was effectively becoming a war to a successful conclusion. Though he did not invent the phrase, it was Templer who popularised the idea of 'hearts and minds', winning the psychological and political war, and the confidence of the bulk of the population.

Mike Calvert was reluctantly invalided back to Britain with a colourful selection of tropical diseases in August 1951, and was succeeded in command by Lieutenant Colonel John Sloane of the Argyll and Sutherland Highlanders. Though inexperienced for the task to which he had been called, he quickly appreciated that the SAS was in danger of working its way out of a job, and back into history. Thus it was that he looked towards a broadening of its capabilities and a usefulness beyond the jungles of Malaya. In the latter part of 1951, the Regiment retrained and reorganised,

dropped its Malayan Scouts prefix, and became known as 22nd Special Air Service Regiment. It was also during the course of 1951 that the SAS winged dagger cap badge was readopted, albeit usually on a red Parachute Regiment beret. By now the establishment allowed was a total of 480 all ranks, including attached corps specialists. This total was divided into four squadrons, one Rhodesian and three British, and a headquarters. The teeth of each squadron was its four Troops, a Troop being an officer and 14 men.

A technique developed during the latter part of 1951 was 'tree jumping'. Insertion on foot could take days of toil through jungle carrying heavy loads. So it was, as in the early days of the Second World War, that the Regiment began experiments with parachutes. The jungle, however, presented very special problems, since there were few clearings sufficiently large to make good parachute landing sites, and these might well be open to enemy observation, or surrounded by dangerous bamboo. The answer appeared to be jumping straight into the canopy of the trees, which had in any case already occurred accidentally, and make a descent from there. A small party under Major Freddy Templer (cousin of the General) began experiments in Selangor, and though there were accidents in which parachutes either slipped

Men of Peter de la Billière's former regiment, the Durham Light Infantry, in Borneo, 1966. The same jungle green uniforms, headgear, and AR 15 (M 16) rifles were also used by the SAS in this campaign.

straight through the trees, or shifted after snagging, a special harness was devised. This could be used in conjunction with a webbing strap or rope, by means of which the parachutist could lower himself to the ground.

In January 1952, Operation Helsby saw the SAS committed to the Belum Valley near the Thai border where it was suspected that the Communist XII Regiment had a company and a headquarters. C and D Squadrons were moved up as far as possible by truck then marched laboriously into position over difficult terrain and swollen rivers. B Squadron were dropped in by parachute, a difficult drop zone and bad weather allowing only four of its 54 men to land directly on target. Nevertheless, the Squadrons sorted themselves out and launched aggressive patrols which soon resulted in a number of contacts and the capture of a terrorist. The civilian population of the valley was later evacuated.

On the basis of this small success, the SAS went on to develop new tactics and clear new and larger areas of the jungle. Helicopter insertion and evacuation were pioneered, and in many operations jungle forts were established in which the native populations could be separated and protected from the Communists. Operations lasted longer, and were re-supplied *in situ*. New jungle patrol tactics were also evolved which saw the extensive use of shotguns and the Patchett carbine (precursor of the Sterling sub-machine gun), relatively short range, high power weapons, suitable for close engagement in the jungle. The SAS were also one of the first units to combine the advantages of shotgun and sub-machine gun, experimenting with the so-called shot gun sight rib on the Patchett – a device intended to improve aiming at fleeting targets.

TERRORIST AMBUSH

In Pahang, during Operation Galway of October 1953 to June 1954, 'hearts and minds' were put to a severe test. Terrorists, who had established themselves amongst a group of local aborigines, opened fire on a troop of B Squadron, killing Lieutenant Fotheringham. The SAS wisely avoided shooting on the jungle dwellers, and were subsequently able to gain their confidence. The Regiment also issued specific instructions that locals should be paid for work or materials supplied, and its medics gave treatment to those who required it. In many ways, 1953 proved a hard year for the Regiment, and it suffered 11 fatalities, the largest yearly total of the whole Malayan emergency.

In Operation Termite in 1954, the Regiment were imaginatively used in conjunction with RAF bombing, two squadrons being dropped into the clearings made by the bombs. In the event, it was determined that bombing jungle achieved relatively little, but that SAS units in squadron strength were effective. Termite led to only 15 confirmed Communist kills, but was a valuable learning exercise. The years 1953 to 1955 also saw considerable changes in terms of organisation and personnel. A fifth Parachute Regiment squadron was attached, and a New Zealand squadron was brought in to replace the Rhodesians, who had left some time earlier. Lieutenant Colonel Sloane was replaced by Oliver Brooke, who was himself injured in a parachute jump, and later replaced by Lieutenant Colonel George Lee.

By 1955, the Communists were slowly losing the conflict, and security force casualties were declining. The Regiment suffered no fatalities that year despite taking part in six operations, and obtaining no fewer than 12 mentions in dispatches. A form of political accommodation would be reached in 1957 when Malaysia was given independence within a Commonwealth framework; even so there were still plenty of combat operations. The Regiment was especially active during the period of May 1956 to December 1957 when it was employed on Operation Gabes North, which involved first B Squadron, then D, and parts

Opposite, **An SAS brew in the Borneo jungle. The weapon, which does not leave the soldier's side, is an M 16. The hot drink is achieved using a small folding hexamine cooker with a metal container of water on top, and all evidence will be cleared away afterwards. The enemy are unlikely to be near, since fires and cigarette smoke would compromise the patrol.** *SAS Association*

of A. It was during this sweep that Sergeant G.R.Turnbull had his celebrated encounter with four Communist terrorists and killed three with his shotgun, wounding the fourth. It was also Turnbull who killed the enemy leader Ah Tuk. He was awarded a Military Medal.

Another character to come to the fore in the latter part of the conflict was the young officer Peter de la Billière, who reached Malaya in 1956, and was later prominent in the tracking of the Ah Hoi gang in the Telok Anson swamp. By this time, much had been learned of jungle skills. According to de la Billière, Bergens were now being carried containing a moderately standard two-week ration, thus allowing patrols to operate independently for a significant period. This vital, though unexciting, Woodhouse Ration comprised seven tins of corned 'Bully' beef, 4 lb of rice, 3 lb of sugar, 10 packets of Army biscuits, 20 Oxo cubes, dried soup, Ovaltine tablets, half a pound each of tea, cheese and potato powder, a little egg powder, and 1 lb of oatmeal. To these basics, individual troopers would add a few extras, such as salt, curry powder, spices or onions to make the food more appetising. As was so often the case, weight was the ultimate limiting factor. A soldier still had to carry such essentials as weapons, ammunition, and a poncho, yet remain mobile enough to be an effective fighter.

SAS methods and ways of command had also developed, as de la Billière relates: 'To be thrown into the jungle with people as independent as these [SAS] was no easy assignment. We wore no badges of rank. There were no other officers from whom I could seek advice or support. There was no mess into which I could escape. Like it or not, I had to live with my Troop for the next 14 weeks. I realised that the only thing to do was communicate with them as much as possible… In talking things through, I unconsciously promoted the SAS tradition of Chinese parliaments – pow wows in which everyone has his say about a problem before the commander takes a decision.'

By the time the last of what was now the regular 22nd SAS left Malaya, it had suffered 28 fatalities, but had inflicted four times this number on the enemy, and helped to bring to a satisfactory end a war which was essentially a no-win situation. Perhaps more importantly, in terms of its own survival, it had proved its unique worth. So it was that although, it was temporarily reduced to just two squadrons (A and D), it would become a permanent peace time feature of the order of battle. For a few months, the Regiment's new UK base would be at Malvern, but by mid-1960 it was at Hereford, Bradbury Lines. Its home headquarters has been there ever since, though the facilities have much improved, and in 1984 the name was changed, fittingly, to Stirling Lines. The shadowy 23rd SAS Regiment Territorials were also raised in 1959, using, it is said, M19 personnel. Formed in London, 23rd SAS was later moved to the Midlands.

TROUBLE IN OMAN

Whilst some of the British Army were lucky enough to return to the UK, it was Major Johnny Watts' D Squadron of the SAS which drew the short straw, being moved direct from one conflict to another, and the shock of being transplanted from the jungles of Malaya to the arid Middle Eastern state of Oman can scarcely be overstated. Not only did the men have to acclimatise themselves to dry heat, but the relatively open terrain and mountainous slopes necessitated a complete revision of weapons and tactics. Short range shotguns and carbines were rapidly jettisoned, and D Squadron began to practice with the new, powerful, and relatively long range self loading rifle. Mules were also adopted for carrying supplies, though many problems were experienced with the cheap and weedy beasts that the government had shipped in from Somalia.

The Oman operation was kept quiet for some time, and for good reason. Britain's prestige was at a low ebb after Suez, and the job of the Regiment in Oman was delicate. Rebel forces led by Talib bin Ali had seized the plateau of Jebel Akhdar and threatened not only the friendly, if medieval, regime of the Sultan, but potentially much of the oil supply of the free world which had to traverse the nearby Straits of Hormuz. On the face of it, D Squadron's job was next to impossible. They had little more than 60 men in an inhospitable country, whilst the enemy or *adoo*, was more than 500 strong and lodged about 8,000 feet above sea level, in a fortress-like position. Moreover, though some of the men of the Talib had only single-shot Martini-Henry rifles, most had much more modern arms like the Lee-Enfield, and a good number of modern support weapons including .5-inch Browning heavy machine guns and mortars. The *adoo* also had mines and snipers, were prepared to launch forays out of their mountain lair, and could make road movement difficult even away from the plateau.

Yet the SAS were not without resource. Surprise would be the best weapon, but there were other factors which could help even the odds. A couple of .30 Browning machine guns were soon talked out of the small Life Guards detachment based in Oman, there were 3.5 inch rocket launchers available, and there was some air support. The Regiment also had a determined leader in the shape of Lieutenant Colonel Tony Deane-Drummond. A measure of the man was given by his strange nickname, 'the Cupboard'. This had come about because Deane-Drummond had hidden in a cupboard for 13 days after the battle of Arnhem rather than surrender himself to the Germans. The Sultan also had limited forces of his own, and though these had not proved capable of taking on the rebels on an even footing, they could be used in a supporting role.

The campaign had an inauspicious start. On 26 November, a 19 Troop patrol, led by 'Tanky' Smith encountered the enemy, as was related by de la Billière: 'Smith saw a single Arab coming up the *wadi* from below, hallooing to his comrades in the rocks above. Tanky waited till the man was within 200 yards, gave him a wave to bring him to a halt, and shot him dead… That one quick fusillade brought the mountain to life. About 20 rebels opened up, and bullets flew in all directions. The second patrol were some 600 yards away, and when they heard the disturbance, prepared to move over to give covering fire; but as one of them, Corporal Duke Swindells, stood up , he was instantly shot in the chest by a rebel hidden in the rocks only 200 yards below him. Swindells died within half a minute…'.

After this, it was all too obvious that the Regiment would have to move by night and by stealth. Over the next month, cautious probes and raids into the mountains discovered that it was possible to get onto the Jebel Akhdar, and that, given the right tactics, the *adoo* could well be defeated in the fire fight. Captain de la Billière led a night patrol which succeeded in creeping up on an enemy post in some caves, and shooting up the *adoo* with rocket launchers, a Browning machine gun and rifle fire, before pulling out. On 27 December, Captain Rory Walker led two Troops up the cliffs on ropes, and though discovered, was able to throw a lucky grenade which cleared the path. His men swarmed boldly up the rocks and succeeded in killing nine of the enemy. Other missions took, and briefly held, parts of the high ground.

With the *adoo* shaken by the SAS and by air raids, and routes identified onto the plateau, the decision was taken to make the decisive strike. To do this, A Squadron were moved into Oman in January 1959, thereby doubling SAS strength, and an all-out assault was planned for after dark on 26 January. The main attack was planned to coincide with a diversionary raid, and an air strike. The SAS climbed all night in silence, bypassing a sleeping enemy machine gun crew, but were short of the top of the Jebel by dawn. Rather than risk being caught below the summit, overlooked by the *adoo*, in broad daylight, a group of SAS men dropped off their Bergens and struck out for the top. Though there was some firing, the enemy was taken entirely by surprise and fled. An air drop re-supplied the men atop the Jebel, and the campaign was effectively decided by a single *coup de main*. Eight mortars and 18 machine guns were captured. The SAS had just two fatalities. The first Oman campaign had been won for a total cost to the Regiment of three lives.

REBELLION IN BORNEO

Like Oman, the war in Borneo was a low profile operation, which had its origins in a rebellion against a sultan. Unlike the first campaign in Oman, however, the struggle was protracted, and as far as the Regiment was concerned, waged largely in the jungles against the army of a third power in the shape of President Sukarno's Indonesia. The Borneo campaign would also stretch the resources of the two squadrons of the SAS to the limit. Brunei was one of three former British colonies which occupied the northern third of the island of Borneo, the remainder of which was the Kalimantan province of Indonesia. It was the revolt in Brunei in December 1962 which gave Indonesia an opportunity to intervene in the hope that the whole island might one day become part of a larger Indonesia.

It would be the job of 22nd SAS, now commanded by Lieutenant Colonel John Woodhouse, to attempt to maintain the integrity of Brunei's 900-mile border, whilst watching their backs against any internal insurgency. Since the Regiment was now so thinly stretched, it was proposed that it be deployed one Squadron at a time, and rotated in four-month tours, depending on the duration of hostilities. So dire was the SAS manpower situation that the revival of two squadrons dissolved at the end of the Malayan emergency was approved, though these new troops were not available immediately.

River boat transport with Bergen. In jungle conditions, rivers are often a faster way to get around than along tracks, and boats leave little or no evidence of their passing. In Borneo, the SAS carried out river ambushes stopping enemy supply.

One of the new squadrons would be a reincarnation of B Squadron, the other a Guards G Squadron.

One early suggestion was that the SAS should parachute into the jungle where and when required, but the Malayan experience of the dangers of parachuting in jungles, combined with the desire to win the 'hearts and minds' of the jungle dwellers at the earliest opportunity, influenced Woodhouse to support a less dramatic pedestrian approach. It was also true that, if patrols were able to spend an appreciable part of their time actually on the ground in the jungle, they would stand the best chance of gleaning valuable intelligence.

A Squadron arrived in January 1963, and soon began to evolve a workable *modus operandi* for a big job with precious few resources. Before long, they had taken to living and watching in four-man patrols, widely spread, but in close contact with the jungle tribesmen. The SAS would not only observe from vantage points, and check tracks for use, but make a deliberate policy of dispensing medical help, and sometimes food, to the locals. From these, they would learn of unusual activity, or the presence of Indonesian troops. So it was that each team managed to cover a border frontage of as much as five or six miles. A vital part of moving about the jungle was trying to make sure that no tell-tale signs were left behind, but as Pete Scholey observed: 'We carried all our rubbish with us. If you buried cans or whatever, the pigs would dig them up. We tried not to leave signs but you always do. It's impossible not to. That's why we avoided tracks and tried whenever possible to penetrate parts of the jungle that even the Abos and the most determined Indos would avoid.'

Though there were experiments with civilian costume, this was decided to be both superfluous and slightly ridiculous, so the troopers lived and fought in jungle green denims with appropriate soft jungle hats. According to one account, these hats were given yellow identifying marks to distinguish the wearers from the similarly-clad Indonesians. Most of the SAS were now using the 7.62 mm self loading rifle, a powerful semi-automatic with a 20-round magazine, perfectly capable of shooting through the trunks of the smaller jungle trees. The SLR was a good weapon, with a range more than adequate for the claustrophobic spaces of the jungle, but it was really quite big and heavy for the purpose. Bren guns were also used on occasion, but these were often an overkill for the situation. The handier US Armalite rifles were gradually introduced as the campaign went on, though at first they were very few and far between.

When warned that a significant enemy movement

Helicopter landing in a jungle clearing provided by SAS and tribesmen. In Borneo, much of the Regiment's work comprised locating the opposition, then making landing zones, so that other British forces could be re-deployed to the vital spot.

was in progress, the SAS team would employ tribesmen to help clear enough ground to allow a helicopter landing. Gurkha troops could then be flown in to set up a blocking position or ambushes. Eventually, as these tactics began to pay dividends, SAS patrols became more aggressive, even crossing the border to locate concentrations of the enemy.

Though intelligence gathering was the prime objective, there were still targets of opportunity. One engagement was recorded by Don Large, whose patrol had been detailed to watch a river for launches and military traffic: 'I was beginning to think of tomorrow's luck when suddenly it was there. It was coming steadily upstream, a big one, at least 40 feet long. Canvas drapes were rolled down at the sides because of the rain, so I couldn't see the cargo. As it passed me I saw a man in jungle green sitting as you often see the troops in the back of army lorries. The thumb went up, and the patrol hit their firing positions. I sprang to my fire position and took out the two men visible at the back of the boat, then put five shots into the cargo compartment to keep that happy.

'The patrol was firing steadily, hitting the flat stern of the boat, centre of the water line. Pete was having trouble with that bloody rifle [the patrol were using self loading rifles]. I watched him go through the drills, trying to clear the problem, then I put another five shots in the boat to keep them busy… The boat slowed and lost way, smoke began to billow from the darkness under the canvas roof. I spaced six rounds across the target area, then changed the magazine… I yelled "Stop!" and that was it, we were on our way.'

Ideally, when the SAS struck, it would be as part of a larger body, backed by the Gurkhas. In one instance, 2/7th Gurkha Rifles actually succeeded in creeping up to an enemy encampment, where the Indonesian troops were rudely interrupted at breakfast by a 3.5 inch rocket and a fusillade of small arms fire. On other occasions, the SAS

improved their chances of a successful ambush by laying electronically detonated claymore mines to blast the head and tail of a section of track, and would focus rifles and machine weapons on the killing zone between.

Once in a while it was the enemy who managed to lure the SAS into a trap, and perhaps the most famous instance of this was the so-called Lillico patrol of February 1965. As the patrol scouted an enemy camp, they were ambushed, and Sergeant Eddie Lillico and Trooper Ian Thomson were both badly hit, whilst the remainder of the patrol were lucky to make good their escape to summon support. Thomson crawled away over 1,000 yards, managing to fire back periodically at any pursuers. As he put it: 'I was watching my life pumping out of me… There were bullets flying everywhere, so I forced myself to move… As I crawled, the shattered bones of my femur were grinding against each other'. Fashioning a makeshift tourniquet with his face veil and Commando knife, he carried on, moving on 'autopilot'. Lillico also survived, though shot right through the pelvis. He passed out, and was on his own for two days in an enemy-infested area. He was eventually winched to safety by a rescue helicopter, and was subsequently awarded a Military Medal for his fortitude.

In the end the war was not so much won, as forced to a conclusion by the collapse of the Indonesian regime, and a settlement was reached in August 1966. The SAS had performed another remarkable task, for a loss of just seven men. A number of medals and mentions in dispatches were made. Peter de la Billière gained a bar to his Military Cross.

SAS RORKE'S DRIFT

Given the near constant involvement of the SAS in action from Malaya onwards, it is perhaps unsurprising that another small war was brewing even before Borneo was at peace. In April 1964, A Squadron was in theory enjoying a respite between Borneo tours with the possibility of some desert training to keep them sharp for the eventuality that they might again be needed in the Middle East at some future date. The place chosen for this training was the trouble spot of Aden, but it just so happened that offensive action was already planned for the Radfan Mountains just to the north, where there was both unrest and threat from the Yemen. It seemed all too natural that the presence of SAS troops should be capitalised on, and so it was that A Squadron was added to the expedition into the Radfan.

The purpose of this venture was defined by the General Officer Commanding Middle East Land Forces as the suppression of the activities of dissidents in the area, an ending of attacks on the Dhala road, and an attempt to nip in the bud the spreading of tribal revolt. Intelligence was patchy, and arguably the Radfan plan was ill thought out. Certainly this was not the kind of defensive 'hearts and minds' operation that had been so successfully mounted in Malaya and Borneo. As if to underline this point, the first exchange of fire involving the SAS was a 'blue on blue' encounter with other British troops.

Things went from bad to worse with the ill-fated Edwards patrol. During April 1964, a nine-man SAS patrol commanded by Captain Robin Edwards was taken up Wadi Rabwa by armoured cars with a view to establishing drop zones for the insertion of parachute forces. Though shot at on the way in, Edwards proceeded with the mission, only to be dogged by further bad luck. His signaller Trooper Warburton was taken ill, and the decision was taken to lay up in some stone *sangars* until the man was fit to carry on. They were discovered by hostile tribesmen from a nearby village and a vicious fire fight commenced. It appeared almost inevitable that Edwards' men would be overcome, but timely intervention from RAF ground attack helped the SAS men hold off a far superior number of the enemy.

As dusk fell, with two men wounded and Warburton dead by tribesmen's bullets, Edwards realised that in darkness, without air cover, his patrol was almost certain to be overcome. He therefore decided to call down an artillery barrage around his position, smash all equipment that could not easily be carried away, and make a break for it. This they did at the run, making fire and movement bounds, and attempting to cover their wounded who hobbled off as best they could. Remarkably everyone but Edwards made it away, though they were pursued vigorously, and were exchanging shots for some hours afterwards. In a macabre postscript, the heads of the two dead men were later exhibited in the Yemen, a total shock to those who were unaware the Regiment were even fighting in the country.

After the initial Radfan expedition, the Regiment continued to be involved in Arabia. In Aden itself undercover operations were undertaken in the hope of undermining Arab nationalist activities. These covert 'Keeni-Meeni' actions were particularly tricky since they took place in a predominantly urban environment, and it was not easy for SAS men to pass themselves off as Arabs. Furthermore, Britain had announced her intention to leave, so there was no long-term goal to be achieved. SAS men were also deployed to the Radfan again, where their tasks included not only patrols but observation and the direction of artillery.

DHOFARI TRIBESMEN

An unusual period of relative peace during the late 1960s was rudely interrupted by a fresh round of unrest in Oman, where the Sultan's iron rule and outside influences conspired to cause Marxist rebellion. The Dhofari tribesmen, some of whom had received training in Iraq, had been restless for some time, but the triggers for SAS deployment were the *coup* which replaced the old Sultan Sa'id with Sultan Qaboos and the Labour Government's announcement that Britain would be withdrawing from the Arabian Gulf. The objectives of Operation

Storm in 1970 were therefore multi-faceted, and by no means purely military. Intelligence gathering, protection of the new Sultan, and counter insurgency were to be mixed with a programme of medical aid and attempting to win over the rebels to the new and more enlightened regime.

The first Troop into Salalah in Oman were involved as much in farming and civil engineering as in intelligence. An official front was maintained that any SAS presence was purely for training. A promising sign was that a split in the rebel movement caused many of the warring tribesmen to seek amnesty, and some of these were recruited into militia units, or *firqas* serving on the

government side. From 1971, the Regiment would take on a more pro-active role, training the *firqas*, and moving into areas hitherto dominated by the rebels. That October, two squadrons were committed to Operation Jaguar in the Jibjat area, and one SAS man was killed in action. The next few years would see other skirmishes, but it was the battle of Mirbat in July 1972 which would go down in regimental annals as the most important.

At this time, Mirbat on the Omani coast consisted of two small forts, a village, and the British Army Training Team, or 'BATT', house. Here a group of nine SAS men from B Squadron were engaged in training the *firqas*, whilst a group of the local Dhofar

An SAS man liaises with locals, Aden. Some of the Regiment's greatest successes have been won by 'hearts and minds'. The weapon is the 7.62 mm self loading rifle.

Gendarmerie were mainly employed in defending the settlement. In all, the SAS could count upon rather less than 100 men with rifles, light machine guns, and one 25 pounder field gun. There had been no major contact with the enemy, though the base had been shelled a couple of times in recent months. The fight which broke out before dawn on 19 July therefore came as a considerable shock.

About a kilometre outside the town, a small patrol of Dhofar Gendarmes was surprised and four killed in a hail of rounds from a 12.7 mm heavy machine gun. Hearing the noise, SAS Captain Mike Kealy rushed to the roof of the fort and observed groups of armed men running towards the BATT house as a mortar barrage came down. A battle which has been compared to Rorke's Drift now began. Whilst the Gendarmes defended their fort, the SAS raced to their positions, manning as many of the critical support weapons as was possible with their meagre numbers. On the roof of the BATT house, Kealy and four other men manned two machine guns, a Browning and a GPMG, whilst SAS Lance Corporal 'Fuzz' Harris fired an 81 mm mortar from a pit nearby. Fijian SAS Corporal Labalaba and another Fijian, Takesavi, manned the 25 pounder alongside Omani gunners.

These weapons did considerable damage to the 250 adoo who were assaulting Mirbat, but they were coming on with determination and were using an 84 mm Carl Gustav anti-tank weapon to good effect against the buildings. They had also got so close so quickly that the mortar had to be lifted off its legs to achieve the necessary elevation to hit the targets. At the gun position things were hectic, and Labalaba was wounded. As his colleague later reported: 'It was ridiculous. They were almost on top of us, shooting from all directions. At least we could hear on the radio that our comrades back in the house were still okay. It was getting very, very fierce, and Laba and I were joking in Fijian. All the fear seemed to go away. We knew the gun was their main target

and we were still firing at point blank range. We had no time to aim. All we could do was pick up a round, load it in and fire as quickly as we could. But the guerrillas were coming closer and closer towards us, and at the end we had to abandon it. You can't fire a 25 pounder at 50 metres. You'd just get metal fragments in your face. And we had to cover ourselves. I heard the crack of a gun. Something hit my shoulder and the shock knocked me out for a few seconds… The clearest way of describing it is like an elephant charging at you at 120 miles an hour… Laba, still bleeding… crawled across to give me a shell dressing.'

Kealy radioed for an air strike, and followed this with a request for helicopter evacuation for the casualties. Taking advantage of a lull, Kealy and Trooper Tobin scurried over to the gun position, covered by the machine gunners, to give aid and bolster the defence. Here they found the two Fijian SAS men still fighting, though both were wounded. An Omani gunner was also wounded, and a couple of Gendarmes were also killed or wounded.

Now the enemy came on again. Things were desperate as the adoo began to overrun the position. Labalaba was shot dead, Tobin wounded, and grenades were thrown into the gun pit. Kealy had shot a couple of the enemy, but just when all appeared hopeless the strike planes arrived. Ground attacks riddled many of the adoo and Kealy survived. Not long after, SAS reinforcements from G Squadron began to appear by helicopter, immediately launching aggressive patrols which drove off the demoralised adoo. By mid-morning the battle was all but over.

Though Trooper Tobin later died, the defenders had acquitted themselves magnificently, accounting for more than 30 of the enemy. Mirbat was undoubtedly the most vicious engagement of the Oman campaign, but it was not the only one. In all, 12 SAS men died in Oman in the period 1971 to 1975, and peace was only finally achieved between Oman and South Yemen in 1976.

MAKING THE SAS

Opposite, **The reality of a 40 lb Bergen on a long distance 'tab' across rough terrain. The Denision smock has given way to more modern mountain and hiking garments, and the Number 4 rifle to more recent weapons.**

In the early days, joining the SAS was a highly informal process, and for officers it was very much a matter of introduction. In 1943, Roy Farran obtained an interview through General Willoughby Norrie: 'We were summoned to a very unconventional type of interview which rather took the wind out of my sails. An interesting looking soldier, who was introduced as Lord Jellicoe, continued to discuss a map in the corner of the room with someone else whose name I cannot remember. During the interview I tried to get a squint over his shoulder and thought it was a map of Sardinia but could not be sure. Bill Stirling [David's brother] was a great and mountainous man, who shook us by the hand and asked us a few embarrassing questions. He radiated an encouraging aura of confidence and, although he told us we would be on a fortnight's trial, we already felt ourselves part of the team before the interview was finished. It was not terminated by the usual abrupt dismissal, but after inviting us to lunch, he turned to discuss highly secret matters with Jellicoe.'

The procedure for other ranks was scarcely better established at this time, though taking the initial recruits from the Commandos, and thereafter selecting from volunteers from other regiments, was some indicator of potential quality. According to General Dempsey, as early as 1943 the success of the regiment was based on six factors: serious training, discipline, physical fitness, confidence but not over confidence, careful planning, and the 'right spirit'. It was a system which usually worked, but there were occasional and sometimes spectacular failures, as when Douglas Berneville-Claye, alias Lord Charlesworth, quit A Squadron, and joined the Waffen SS!

Since then, with increased professionalism, increased competition, and shrinkage of the Army, recruitment has changed out of all recognition. A significant step forward was the introduction of a dedicated programme designed by Major John Woodhouse in 1953. Woodhouse, later the Regiment's commanding officer, was a Second World War veteran with a Military Cross to his credit. His appearance was described by Peter de la Billière as 'not particularly impressive, having a slender gangling figure and what we called a "Bergen stoop"; but his reputation was that of an outstanding leader who always drove himself to his limits, put the welfare of his men before his own, and expected the highest standards from everyone. His renown was enough to make any recruit nervous.' Yet Woodhouse also worked by example, temporarily exchanging identities with one of his men, and taking part on an equal footing in some of the exercises that he had helped to devise. In the 1950s, initial selection lasted only two weeks, even so it was tough enough. De la Billière, who took part in 1956, described carrying packs weighted to 55 lb, falling asleep on his feet, vomiting his breakfast due to exertion, losing over a stone in weight, a feeling of unpredictability, and pouring rain which sapped morale 'to its lowest ebb'.

SAS SELECTION

There are now two formal courses each year, winter and summer, each of which lasts four weeks and accommodates about 150 potential candidates who have applied from their existing parent regiments. Winter courses are sometimes thought the hardest due to sleet and cold, but the summer can mean more undergrowth, making running very difficult. Any male member of the British Armed Forces may apply to join, provided that they have more than three years left to serve, and, if they are officers, they are aged between 22 and 34, or men between 19 and 34.

Yet just putting your name forward can be more harrowing than many people imagine, since the very act of volunteering means scrutiny from colleagues, and opens up the possibility of being regarded as a traitor to one's regiment. This is obviously embarrassing for many, since the majority of would-be SAS men end up 'RTU' – Returned To Unit –

SAS parachutists line
up on a temporary air strip
in Malaya ready to board
Valetta aircraft of RAF
48 Squadron.

MAKING THE SAS

when they fail to make the grade. In theory, only the SAS itself can refuse the application to join, but as Andy McNab observed in the 1980s: 'Some regiments, especially the corps, aren't keen for their men to go because they have skills that are hard to replace. They won't give them time off, or they'll put the application in "File 13" – the waste paper basket. Or they'll allow the man to go but make him work right up till the Friday before he goes'.

Apart from potential humiliation, the candidate also has more practical matters to consider. NCOs joining the Regiment revert to being Troopers, and lose rank. It also used to be the case that such men were worse off financially through joining the Regiment, though this was addressed during the 1980s with the introduction of 'Special Services' pay. Officers face no demotion, but usually stay with the Regiment just three years before being moved on. SAS service may help an officer's career, and has been the stepping stone for several generals, but carries many risks, and in some instances has had detrimental results. Officers may be returned to their units just like the men.

The Regiment also has a particularly pernicious effect on family life: all servicemen expect foreign service, danger, and potentially long separations. For the SAS such service is worse as it has to remain secret, and the Trooper *incommunicado*. The Regiment can become a way of life, and a sort of family in its own right. As one SAS wife put it: 'Many members of the Regiment stay single, or have one failed relationship after another, because the time away from the job is in some ways much harder than anything they face at work. Suddenly they have to deal with real life, real emotions, and learn how not to hurt people's feelings. They can't just be themselves in their own little world looking after Number One. They are not used to demands on their time, attentions, and emotions.' Disincentives, like loss of stripes and separation, are almost part of the selection: those who cannot stomach them are not wanted by the Regiment.

The paper work complete, successful applicants proceed to Hereford for the practical part of the process. Many are shocked by the apparent informality of Stirling Lines. As one put it: 'When you go in through those gates, the frightening thing is the quietness. After the shouting and screaming and bawling I'd been used to, great big blokes… were whispering troop sergeants'. Yet there really is no need for shouting. Any candidate guilty of lateness, or minor insubordination, is sent straight to Platform 4 – the return railway platform out of Hereford and out of SAS selection. As Peter de la Billière has observed, a cornerstone of the SAS is each man's ability to organise himself and accept the greatest possible responsibility at the lowest level. This is in stark contrast with much of the Army where there is minute organisation calculated to prevent anyone putting a single foot wrong.

The course starts easy and gets progressively harder. The first exercise is an ordinary Basic Fitness Test, conducted early in the morning. The 'BFT' is a mile and a half run, in light kit, with boots, taking no more than 11 minutes, straightforward for anyone contemplating being in the Army, let alone the SAS. This is soon followed by the Army Combat Fitness Test, which comprises a nine-mile course, covered in a mixture of running and walking, in combat kit, with webbing and weapon. The load carried is a manageable 25-35 lb. In theory, all active soldiers should be capable of the 'CFT' and the test is a mere warm-up in SAS terms, but surprisingly a percentage of applicants are eliminated even at this stage. Next, the marches get longer and the degree of map reading and orientation required greater. For these, the candidates are taken out by lorry into the Brecon Beacons and Black Mountains of Wales. At one time, the men's packs were filled with bricks. More recently, the loads carried are just as great but are made up of potentially useful stores like food and clothes, rifles are often carried, and must not leave the soldier's side.

An SAS man equipped for 'tree jumping' in Malaya. In addition to the rope for lowering himself from trees, he has a weapon drop bag, and an SAS beret pushed through the webbing of his parachute harness.

With the non-starters out of the way, the field of candidates now comprises some of the fittest and most determined men in the Army. Many will have trained intensively. This was certainly the case with Gaz Hunter who applied in 1977: 'To train for the SAS I went out on the hills, with my weight on my back, alone. I walked and ran for miles in the sun, rain, wind and fog, navigating up, over and down the high, steep, uneven and boggy ground of the Welsh hills: ground where so many leave their hopes behind. I have never trained without navigating. I came to see that a two-minute map study could be worth an hour on the ground. I had to improve my stamina and determination, learn to read the land – and I had to do it on my own. A lot of soldiers who can run for miles fail selection. It's as much about the inner game as it's about stamina and strength.'

This is an important observation since the 'inner game' of attitude and fortitude is actually more important than many candidates appreciate. Mental ability also gets some trials, with odd mathematical or strategic questions thrown into the tests just when they are not expected. Some very fit men are dropped because they express despair, cannot do simple sums, or fail to get on and work as a team. Ian Simpson served as an instructor, and as his wife noted: 'It was part of his job on Training Wing to identify fruitcakes, the macho mule heads who only wanted to join the SAS so that they could jump through windows with all the black kit on. It was his specific task to bin anyone who lost their nerve in the jungle or on the Brecon Beacons or who seemed unstable, people who could jeopardize the lives of a whole Troop through either foolish heroics or cowardice.'

SICKENERS

It is said that in the 1970s exercises were designed specifically as 'Sickeners' – stressful or disgusting things – which would test the man's mental mettle. 'Soldier I' who joined the regiment in 1970 remembered a very special mud crawl:

Opposite, **An exhausted marcher on exercise with non-standard walking boots and trousers, and an old Number 4 bolt action rifle.**

'Tim had saved up the most challenging ordeal for the end. He lined us up and introduced us to the horrors of the entrails trench: a ditch beside a hawthorn hedge, two feet deep, four feet across, filled with stagnant water and rotting sheep's innards. A real cesspit… I took a deep breath and plunged into the foul mess. Two feet doesn't sound very deep, but when you are crawling on all fours so close to the ground it is very deep… Half way across, weighed down by my Bergen, I felt my belt snag on a rock. I couldn't use my hands to free myself as they were holding my rifle clear of the surface. I had to resort to wriggling free by shaking my hips. As I did so I set up a turbulence in the water, and the filthy stinking sheep gut-filled liquid splashed up around my lips. I coughed and spat out in disgust.'

Another psychological ploy used on the same course was to take the men on a long march, then direct them to the transport home, parked a few yards away. Before the recruits reached the Bedfords they started up and drove off.

Many would-be SAS men had their own special wrinkles that they believed would help them through selection. Peter Crossland's advice was not to over train in advance but 'Wait until you start selection, and use the course to bring you to your peak. And never swap food for sleep. Always eat as much as you can stuff into your body, because you will burn calories at a rate of 6000 a day.' One instructor told Andy McNab that two pints of Guinness and a bag of chips was the best prescription each evening. Some men carried chili sauce, curry powder, or salt and pepper to add to monotonous food. Others swore by customized webbing, pads between Bergens and backs or shoulders, socks of particular natural fibres – or two pairs of socks, surgical spirit, oils, or the careful puncturing and covering of blisters. Steve Devereux, viewing his colleagues on the 1982 winter selection, saw men with all sorts of 'magical' things including special compasses 'that light up in the dark', 'go-faster pills', and specially mixed

Next page, **SAS soldiers attend the Royal Marine snipers course.**
Defence Picture Library

'Alpine breakfast'. Mars Bars are perhaps the most perennially popular SAS selection course 'fuel' being compact, and high in calories and sugar, for a rapid and easily digested shot of energy.

For avoiding dehydration during strenuous training, large quantities of water are obviously necessary. Some men think that time can be saved by linking up water bottles to their mouths with tubes, the theory being that liquid may be taken without stopping. Yet such devices are prone to failure, and the tried and trusted method of a bottle for immediate use on the belt kit, with spares in the Bergen has been found to be the best.

The first really big test of the selection course is the legendary 'Fan Dance'. The 'Fan' is in fact Pen y Fan, the highest mountain in the Brecon Beacons. This oval or 'slug shaped' lump said to be 'engraved on every SAS man's heart' is a considerable natural obstacle, having at its western end the Storey Arms Mountain Rescue Centre, and an old Roman road on the east. Steve Devereux described the 'Fan Dance': 'It was a basic, no-nonsense tab with a Bergen weighing 40 lb over a distance of 22 km up, across and down the other side and back... The course was split into two groups, one at either end of the mountain; the two groups were to meet somewhere in the middle, and there was no advantage to starting at any particular end. The Storey Arms end was an almost immediate steep climb, the Torpanto end (the start of the Roman road) a more leisurely looking incline.'

Devereux's own ascent, from the Torpanto end, was conducted at 'blistering pace', in pouring rain, with the candidates struggling to keep up with the 'Directing Staff', or 'DS' non- commissioned officer. Approaching the first steep climb, the rain turned to hail, coming down the Storey Arms end and playing havoc with the knees but there could be no shirking, since the DS took the names of all at the far check-point. Coming back up he again saw hail turn to snow, and Mars Bars frozen into solid blocks, but he made it in good time. A man nicknamed

Top, A crashed Wessex helicopter of 845 Naval Air Squadron on the Fortuna glacier, South Georgia, during the Falklands War. SAS men in snow camouflage are visible in the back ground.

Bottom, Men of Mountain Troop 22 SAS on the Fortuna glacier being approached by a Navy pilot at the moment of rescue. The SAS wear snow camouflage smocks or parkas with fur edged hoods, some have tinted goggles.

Snapper recalled that his ascent of Pen y Fan was interrupted by a member of the DS who belaboured him with mental arithmetic.

ENDURANCE

The 'Fan Dance' usually sees off a good proportion of the candidates, but, as far as the course itself is concerned, merely represents a change of gear. As Gaz Hunter stated: 'We had two more weeks of mountain navigation, over longer and longer distances with ever increasing weight on our backs, alone. The final week was called test week. This was the worst week of all, the marches were all long and with a set weight of 30 kilograms plus all the belt kit and the weapon. Every day that passed was one less to do, that's how I looked at it, every day I was getting nearer to the successful five per cent. We were allowed a part day off before "Endurance", the final test of the first phase of Selection, 64 kilometres in 18 hours with 30 kilograms of weight over the worst country they could find for us.'

Andy McNab recalled that his particular Endurance march was mainly in darkness because it was winter. He thought his Bergen weighed little less than 60 lb because it was packed with extra food and water. He could have chosen to drink from streams and pools but to do so would risk contaminated water and possible failure. Aniseed twists and Yorkie bars were carried for instant energy and morale. During the second night on the move, his torch batteries failed, and he found himself clambering painfully over fallen trees. After 21 hours, he made it back, feet so swollen that he could no longer get into his ordinary shoes. So he cut holes in his trainers, and flapped about like a tramp until his feet recovered. Frank Collins saw a corporal with feet so pulverized by long marches on the selection course that blood appeared at the eyelets of his boots. Understandably, the man gave up at that point.

The toughness of the regime is illustrated by the fact that at least seven men have died on the various long marches of SAS selection over the years, four of them in 1979 and 1980. Perhaps, as Lofty Wiseman's famously black exclamation put it, 'Death is nature's way of telling you that you've failed selection'. Endurance claimed its best-known victim in February 1979, in the shape of Major Mike Kealy, when this veteran of Mirbat joined the novices on the selection course to hone his skills. This particular 40-mile hike commenced at the Talybont reservoir, with snow on the ground, and visibility down to a few yards. Perhaps unwisely, Kealy carried bricks rather than extra supplies of food and clothing to make his Bergen up to the regulation weight, and he pressed on whilst the severe weather conditions were driving others into temporary shelter. Back markers amongst the group offered Kealy gloves and assistance before he dropped behind, and by the time his exhausted state had been realised, and he had been located by rescuers, he was already unconscious. Fog, and the fact that other men were also missing, delayed helicopter airlift off the mountains for 19 hours. Kealy did not survive the ordeal.

Getting through Endurance is a major hurdle, but by no means makes entry into the Regiment a certainty, for it is followed by nearly four months of Continuation Training. By this time, the original course intake is reduced to no more than 30.

Prepared for jungle stalking practice with air rifles and fencing masks, Malaya c.1950. Jungle green uniform, 1944 Pattern webbing, a face veil, and a Number 36 Mills grenade are also in evidence.
IWM MAL303

Continuation Training goes back over many of the basics of soldiering, field craft, rifle and mortar drill, since many of the men who pass selection were formerly in the corps, and therefore not familiar with the latest infantry weapons. These crucial skills confirmed, the men are introduced to explosives and the standard SAS demolition charges, and tested on swimming and language ability. Trials of various types of initiative are thrown in for good measure. At some point in Continuation Training, the recruits also have to undertake a basic parachute jumping course, usually at the Parachute Training School at RAF Brize Norton in Oxfordshire. A standard course is likely to take about four weeks and include eight actual descents. Of these one is from a tethered balloon, one at night, and one from low level.

Continuation not only makes sure that all men are brought up to the same minimum standards, but gives another chance for close scrutiny. Occasionally a man slips through initial selection by brute force and boundless stamina, but inability to work as part of a team, or to grasp the essentials of weapons handling, can still end a man's SAS career at this stage. All the while, the men are watched by eagle-eyed Directing Staff, as much on the look-out for mental failure or instability, as a specific problem with any task. Though it may appear otherwise, relatively few are dropped for a single error. The staff keep notebooks with sections for each man and jot down points for and against. Being dropped is often a cumulative process, an answer back on top of a poor time or an inability to cope with a particular situation can be the final straw. Back at camp there are pictures of the potential recruits and one by one their faces are struck out with a red pen as the losses mount.

JUNGLE TRAINING

The next phase of training is the jungle. For this, the candidates are flown out to Brunei (occasionally Belize) and divided up into patrols, which, following

basic instruction, have both to survive and carry out tasks in an unfamiliar environment of heat and high humidity. A typical Brunei tour lasts about six weeks, two spent in acclimatization and learning jungle skills, two on specialized battle, navigation and survival. Finally, there is a full exercise which usually consists of one half of the squadron taking on the other, patrolling and then attacking the opposition camp.

According to Andy McNab, jungle training is begun around some 'atap' or leaf-covered huts, erected for the purpose by the local Iban tribesmen. The most important of these is the 'Schoolhouse', a simple roof over two rows of log benches. Here the Directing Staff deliver some of the most important lessons of jungle survival. One golden rule is that in the jungle the men always operate as pairs. It is easy to get lost, and the practice of providing cover for each other is a valuable habit to acquire. Almost as important is the instruction that the belt kit, weapon, and 'golock' or machete, accompany the man at all times. Remarkably, Frank Collins even saw an instructor Returned to Unit for leaving his belt kit behind. When the weapon and belt kit are put down nearby, the golock remains physically attached by means of a length of paracord for it is the most essential survival item, providing food and protection.

HALO (High Altitude Low Opening), a form of parachuting used by SAS.
Defence Picture Library

Opposite, SAS soldiers can volunteer for service with air troop skydivers.
Defence Picture Library

To the SAS man, the belt kit is almost a home from home in which he learns to live and work, almost unconsciously. In the early 1950s, the Regiment was issued with 1944 Pattern webbing for use in the Malayan jungle; although lightweight, and dyed jungle green, it was not up to the task. It interfered with the carrying of rucksacks, it was often uncomfortable, and the belt had a tendency to rot or fall apart under the extreme stresses placed upon it. The result was that the troopers extemporized their own kit, using RAF cargo straps, combined with locally made ammunition and ration pouches, and a water bottle. Sometimes parts of the old 1937 Pattern equipment were used, due to its durability. After the introduction of the 1958 Pattern equipment SAS belt, kit became somewhat more uniform, but was still assembled in a way to suit regimental requirements. For many years, until the introduction of the latest 'PLCE' or Personal Load Carrying Equipment, most belt kits consisted of a 1958 Pattern belt supported by two lightweight shoulder straps. On to this was put a low-slung SAS ammunition pouch for four magazines, a pouch containing a prismatic compass, a ration pouch large enough to accommodate a mess tin and a small first aid kit, two 1944-type aluminium water bottles in carriers, and the machete in its scabbard.

Pete Scholey learned much on the course and

SAS parachutists board an aircraft for a drop into the jungle of North Perak, Malaya. Airborne forces helmets and 'tree jumping' ropes are worn.
IWM MAL (C) 370

more later from legendary Korean war veteran 'Lofty' Large. One significant skill he picked up was packing all the necessary equipment into a small space. According to Scholey, the kit for the jungle in addition to weapon, water bottle, and machete, comprised a Swiss Army knife, poncho, everlasting match, magnifying glass, small saw, whistle, signal mirror, signal codes and survival procedures, salt, Oxo cube, sugar, torch, sleeping bag, tin opener with spoon, snare, spare paracord, fish hooks, candle, needle and thread, razor blade, mess tin, suture kit, bandage, sling, and sterilizing tablets. All this he managed to attach in one way or another to his belt kit. Ideally, the kit was stowed in such a way as to keep the front reasonably clear, so as not to impede rapid movement.

In the jungle, two sets of clothing are the usual allowance, one wet and one dry. In theory, the dry set could be kept so by being wrapped up and used as night clothing, and the wet set used in the rain and on the move through wet foliage. In practice, many trainees get drenched and have to stay that way. As Trooper 'Mack' put it: 'Basically you are living in shit. As long as you don't fight it, you can make yourself really comfortable. The first thing I used to do was find myself a suitable position for my bed. It had to be somewhere with good drainage, so usually on a slope and not too far to walk to replenish your water. Then I would set up my pole bed – two long poles which you feed through a piece of canvas with slats folded and stitched running the length of it on either side, so that it looks a bit like an old-fashioned stretcher. How you fix it is up to you, but I preferred being on a high rise, about six feet off the ground, slung between two trees, with my poncho over the top to keep out the worst of the rain. We were still always soaked through.'

For Frank Collins, the jungle was uncomfortable, but neutral: 'The biggest mistake you can make is to treat it like the enemy… Some people never learn… the jungle closes in and suffocates them.

An SAS instructor explains
the rudiments of Communist
weaponry to trainees of
the Parachute Regiment,
Gurkhas, and Signals.
The weapon in the instructor's hands is a Simonov
SKS carbine, a simple and
robust automatic first
manufactured in Russia,
but later produced in China
and elsewhere. The machine
guns on the ground include
a Second World War period
Degtyarev, and a member
of the more modern RPD
family of weapons.

Next page, SAS troops jump
out of a Portuguese Chinook
during cross training.
Defence Picture Library

They have to get out. I find the jungle oppressive but gradually, painfully, I become a part of it. We don't use soap because it smells and we don't shave, we clean our teeth without toothpaste and after a while we begin to look as overgrown and wild as the jungle itself '.

On the jungle course, the men receive fresh food some of the time, but are expected to survive mainly on a mixture of preserved rations and what they can glean from their environment. Important natural resources include the 'jungle cabbage', a sort of small tree with edible pulp, and fish. Catching fish is a skill often taught by the Ibans, and the smaller fish do not need to be gutted but simply cooked whole. Many items, including some types of bark and spider, are also potential food, but even the experts cannot remember each and every one.

The trainees are taught a cautious approach with the unfamiliar. One technique is to rub a little of the proposed meal on the skin or lips and wait a couple of hours to see if there is an untoward reaction. Later, the experiment may be repeated with tongue or gums before eating a little. On operations where issue rations are available jungle food is not often eaten, since a mistake can put a man out of action, and gathering and preparing enough to sustain an active body can take up a considerable time.

INSECTS AND SNAKES

Almost every SAS aspirant is troubled by insects in the jungle. Peter Crossland recalled his experience: 'it was a bit of a shock to me… the whole jungle is teeming with insect life, much of which is attempting to eat you alive. Early one morning

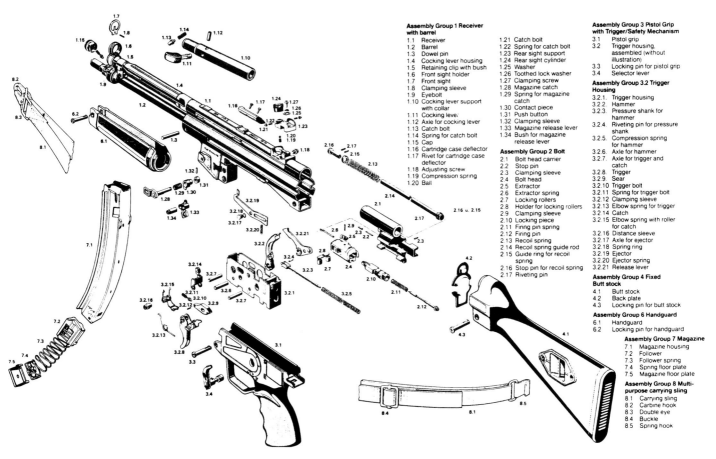

Assembly Group 1 Receiver with barrel			
1.1	Receiver	1.21	Catch bolt
1.2	Barrel	1.22	Spring for catch bolt
1.3	Dowel pin	1.23	Rear sight support
1.4	Cocking lever housing	1.24	Rear sight cylinder
1.5	Retaining clip with bush	1.25	Washer
1.6	Front sight holder	1.26	Toothed lock washer
1.7	Front sight	1.27	Clamping screw
1.8	Clamping sleeve	1.28	Magazine catch
1.9	Eyebolt	1.29	Spring for magazine catch
1.10	Cocking lever support with collar	1.30	Contact piece
1.11	Cocking lever	1.31	Push button
1.12	Axle for cocking lever	1.32	Clamping sleeve
1.13	Catch bolt	1.33	Magazine release lever
1.14	Spring for catch bolt	1.34	Bush for magazine release lever
1.15	Cap		
1.16	Cartridge case deflector	**Assembly Group 2 Bolt**	
1.17	Rivet for cartridge case deflector	2.1	Bolt head carrier
1.18	Adjusting screw	2.2	Stop pin
1.19	Compression spring	2.3	Clamping sleeve
1.20	Ball	2.4	Bolt head
		2.5	Extractor
		2.6	Extractor spring
		2.7	Locking rollers
		2.8	Holder for locking rollers
		2.9	Clamping sleeve
		2.10	Locking piece
		2.11	Firing pin spring
		2.12	Firing pin
		2.13	Recoil spring
		2.14	Recoil spring guide rod
		2.15	Guide ring for recoil spring
		2.16	Stop pin for recoil spring
		2.17	Riveting pin

Assembly Group 3 Pistol Grip with Trigger/Safety Mechanism	
3.1	Pistol grip
3.2	Trigger housing, assembled (without illustration)
3.3	Locking pin for pistol grip
3.4	Selector lever

Assembly Group 3.2 Trigger Housing	
3.2.1	Trigger housing
3.2.2	Hammer
3.2.3	Pressure shank for hammer
3.2.4	Riveting pin for pressure shank
3.2.5	Compression spring for hammer
3.2.6	Axle for hammer
3.2.7	Axle for trigger and catch
3.2.8	Trigger
3.2.9	Sear
3.2.10	Trigger bolt
3.2.11	Spring for trigger bolt
3.2.12	Clamping sleeve
3.2.13	Elbow spring for trigger
3.2.14	Catch
3.2.15	Elbow spring with roller for catch
3.2.16	Distance sleeve
3.2.17	Axle for ejector
3.2.18	Spring ring
3.2.19	Ejector
3.2.20	Ejector spring
3.2.21	Release lever

Assembly Group 4 Fixed Butt stock	
4.1	Butt stock
4.2	Back plate
4.3	Locking pin for butt stock

Assembly Group 6 Handguard	
6.1	Handguard
6.2	Locking pin for handguard

Assembly Group 7 Magazine	
7.1	Magazine housing
7.2	Follower
7.3	Follower spring
7.4	Spring floor plate
7.5	Magazine floor plate

Assembly Group 8 Multi-purpose carrying sling	
8.1	Carrying sling
8.2	Carbine hook
8.3	Double eye
8.4	Buckle
8.5	Spring hook

Diagram of the MP5, 9mm sub-machine gun. Made by Heckler and Koch of Oberndorf-am-Neckar, Germany, the MP 5 is a compact and versatile SAS weapon weighing only 2.5 kg. First adopted by the German police and Border guards, it is now widely used in a number of different variants by military and police forces around the world. The standard model is 680 mm in length, but the telescopic butt MP5 A3 model collapses to 490 mm. The MP5K is shorter still at 325 mm. Having a full automatic cyclic rate of 650 rpm, and the ability to fire accurate single shots from a closed bolt, the MP5 is ideal for most close range purposes.

while it was still dark, I was sitting on my sleeping bag putting some repellent on my boots when some of it accidentally dropped on my groin… Next morning, after a very restless night, I discovered that my testicles had swollen to the size of tennis balls.' Trooper 'Mack' remembered an encounter with a particularly vicious type of bug which bit him whilst asleep, and apparently laid eggs in his neck. The lump had to be cut out by a medic, and the treatment followed up by an intra-muscular injection of penicillin to stop secondary infection.

Johnny 'Two-Combs' faced his particular purgatory when he disturbed a hornets' nest whilst drawing water. The stings were like jabs from a red hot poker and forced him to jump into the stream to escape. Yet he could not leave his rifle and water bottles behind and was forced to retrace his steps. He later suffered from the attention of red ants. McNab was plagued by mosquitoes. Steve Devereux was more worried by the leeches, humidity, and lack of sleep, and lost a stone in weight. Snakes are in a different and potentially lethal category. Trainees are taught a little about them, and that if bitten, they or a comrade should attempt to kill the beast. It can then be shown to medical staff who should then be able to administer the correct antidote.

The more strictly military part of the jungle training centres on such matters as jungle navigation, patrolling, and contact drills. SAS activity in jungles is expected to be in small groups, with intelligence gathering, early warning, reconnaissance, or ambush objectives. For this reason, there is also particular emphasis on teaching how to break off combats, the preparation of helicopter landing zones, and stealthy movement. 'Cross graining' is a particular skill in jungle conditions and entails navigating direct from point to point rather than taking the more obvious routes over high ground or along established tracks. This is slow and labour intensive, but when moving in this way an SAS patrol is highly unlikely to be taken by

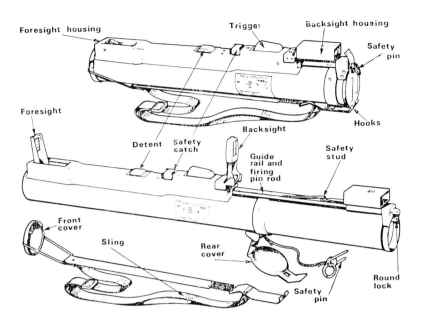

Top, Diagram of the M72, Light Anti-Tank Weapon, in travel and firing modes. Capable of dealing with soft skinned vehicles and most armoured vehicles except the latest main battle tanks, the single shot 66 mm LAW was a mainstay of the SAS arsenal in the Falklands and the Gulf. The HEAT or High Explosive Anti-Tank warhead of the missile can penetrate 305 mm of armour, engaging moving targets at up to 150 m, and stationary targets up to 300 m. In SAS hands, it has often been used as a sort of hand-held howitzer for knocking out buildings and bunkers.

Bottom, Men of the Parachute Regiment on exercise with a 7.62 mm General Purpose Machine Gun, 1969. Firing a powerful round at a cyclic rate of 850 per minute, the GPMG or 'Gimpy' is used by the SAS when heavy firepower is required. It may be used with a bipod, in a tripod mounted support role, or mounted on Land Rovers as in the Gulf. It is interesting to observe that the Parachute Regiment is the largest single source of recruits for the SAS.

Next page, An SAS soldier in Belize runs towards a Lynx Helicopter. *Defence Picture Library*

surprise. In enemy areas, men are taught to move without leaving any signs of their presence and movement becomes even slower. Wood is moved and then moved back again, rather than being cut, cobwebs are left in place and circumvented, obvious footprints are avoided, rubbish is carefully collected and carried away. Even skilled trackers have difficulty in following such a patrol. This type of movement is as much a test of nerve and patience as physical stamina, for the distance covered may be less than a mile a day.

Observation is a critical skill on the jungle course. Sometimes instructors have been known to leave odd pieces of kit, ammunition or mess tins beside the line of march. Questions after the event help identify those who really look at their environment. Observation similarly has a role in booby trapping, and avoiding booby traps. The men learn about traps with sharpened bamboo stakes, mortar bombs hung in trees, and trip wires which may, or may not, be attached to claymore mines.

Jungle stalking skills were, and according to veteran Ken Connor, still are improved by a novel and painful method. The recruits are divided into two groups and issued with air rifles and fencing masks. They then cautiously seek out and track down the opposition, trying to sting them with a pellet before they themselves are detected. Modern technology now makes possible more sophisticated and less risky versions of this method with guns that register electronic or other simulated hits. A couple of different systems were in use with the British Army by 1990. With SAWES – the Small Arms Weapon Effect Simulator system – each man wears a light harness on which are mounted detectors. This MWDS or Man Worn Detector System reacts to simulated fire, produced by low power lasers. Equipping both teams with the SAWES system can produce quite useful fire fight training, umpires being made aware of hits by an alarm which sounds when the lasers strike the detectors. The basic training system is viable to

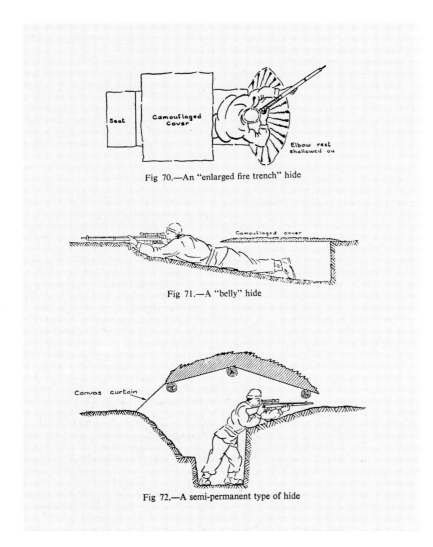

Fig 70.—An "enlarged fire trench" hide

Fig 71.—A "belly" hide

Fig 72.—A semi-permanent type of hide

Left, Different types of sniper cover, as depicted in Infantry Training volume 1, 1951. Such hides make sniping and observation both safer and more comfortable.

Opposite, Unarmed combat Ju-Jitsu style as illustrated by James Hipkiss, 1941. From primitive beginnings in the Great War, unarmed combat would become a familiar feature of military training. It is an integral part of SAS combat and survival.

800 metres, more than enough for most jungle situations, but the SAS will use the real thing whenever possible.

For live firing, the instructors will often prepare what are known as 'jungle lines'. These are usually strips of ground alongside a river, over which the trainees will have to advance as individuals or patrols whilst keeping alert. At various vantage points, the instructors will have placed static targets which have to be engaged or avoided. Elsewhere, there will be pop-up targets which will suddenly appear and be fired on. The skill is not just to identify the wood and cardboard enemy and shoot them, but how to advance and retire, how to shoot quickly, and where to rally after making an escape. Contrary to popular belief, such training is by no means new; similar methods were used as early as the Great War for snipers, and in America's Hogan's Alley for the training of law enforcement.

According to Frank Collins, such jungle drill could be equally applicable to grenades as small arms: 'Our combat drills put all the pressures on us that we would expect in a real battle. As a patrol we advance down a valley, knowing the enemy's out there. Suddenly, a target pops up. We're an aggressive, reactive patrol, and we have to take out the target. As we advance we use our grenades. Our lead scout fires off. As bullets fly, the shout goes up, "Enemy right!" The patrol leader directs us, "Frank, move round!" Then there's a yell, "Grenades!" The rest of the Army hardly ever uses grenades in this way. If they throw a grenade they watch where it lands and then get their heads down… we hit the deck and then we're up running forward almost immediately, firing on automatic as we go… no wonder the SAS often has training fatalities. The weapons and ammo we're using are all real.'

COMBAT SURVIVAL

Back in the UK, the SAS candidate faces his final obstacle, the combat survival course. This is an intensive three-week period intended to enable men to survive and fight behind enemy lines, and prepare them for the possibility of capture and interrogation. Unlike many parts of the SAS man's selection and training, the survival course is also attended by members of other services, and the participants may include Marines and air crew, sometimes even placements from abroad and women. Mike Curtis recalled being put in a small group for part of the course which comprised two SAS candidates, two RAF men, and an Italian.

Part of the course is held at Hereford, where the teaching focuses on survival techniques. Here the trainees learn what plant life, seaweed, and fungus are edible. They also contrive to make 'bashas' or

Fig. 56
(a) Step forward and drop simultaneously. Keep close to him.

Fig. 57
(b) Pivot on *left* knee and throw all your weight against his thigh.

Fig. 58
Keep your back *flat*. Bend forward from your hips.

shelters from wood, sacking, and other detritus. Frank Collins remembered making particularly fetching headgear out of an old fertilizer bag. The instructors for this part of the course include not only the usual Directing Staff but ex- prisoners of war, gardening experts, and poachers.

Learning to catch and kill animals for food is also a significant part of the proceedings. Much of the work is theoretical, especially where snares and traps are concerned, and there is also a section on fishing. Yet Andy McNab recalled a session with chickens which was at once both practical and farcical. The trainees were stationed at the bottom of a hill and one of the instructors opened a large

crate of fowl at the top. The class had to chase the birds and catch and kill them with their bare hands. McNab decided the best way was to remove his jacket and throw it over the startled chicken, which was then killed and later roasted in the fire. Frank Collins got some experience with seagulls, squirrels, and cabbages, before the more civilized procedure of roasting acorns to make a drink vaguely resembling coffee.

A potentially nerve-wracking section of the course relates to guard dogs. Handlers demonstrate what dogs can do, and some of the candidates have to find out what it is like to be pursued by them, protected only by an arm pad. Steve Devereux had a particularly difficult time on this part of the course:

'I ran for about 20 metres before this 110 pound Alsatian came leaping up at me. Instead of going for my protected arm, it ripped through my DPMs [camouflage combats] and bit me on the arse. To make matters worse, I could hear the handler encouraging his dog, so I was livid. I managed to turn around and face the class and present my covered arm to the animal which it accepted. Its jaw locked over my arm; thankfully I felt no teeth. With the animal on my arm, I… bashed the dog's nose with my clenched right fist. The force made the dog loosen its grip on my arm and sink its teeth into my right thigh. The joke was now over and I was deadly serious. I didn't dare move for fear that the dog would do more damage. I just screamed at the handler that if he did not call the dog off, I would rip its jaws open and do the same for him… I had very nasty wounds… which had to be treated immediately.'

The climax of the survival course is a big escape and evasion exercise, run by the Joint Services Interrogation Wing, often on Exmoor, but sometimes at other fittingly bleak locations. For this, the candidates part with their uniform and equipment, being issued instead with some old battle dress, a great coat which often lacks buttons and dates back to the 1950s, boots, and a few pence in loose

An SAS soldier holding an Armalite rifle.
Defence Picture Library

change. All of the clothing has seen better days, holes and stains are usual, missing portions and absent boot laces not unknown. If you are very lucky you may also get an escaper's button compass, a blade and fish hooks stored in an old tobacco tin, or a small silk map. Sometimes men try to secrete food, a knife, or extra money, but this is usually discovered and confiscated during a strip search at the commencement of the exercise, during which every cavity is examined. One ploy which occasionally works is recorded by Peter Crossland: 'Many of the lads fold a £20 note as small as possible, then put it in a condom and swallow it. Normally it will pass through the system in about 24 hours. A good mate of mine tried this – unfortunately he didn't see it again until after the exercise was over'.

Once searched, the participants are released, perhaps with a series of rendezvous points to follow representing moves down an escape line, or a jerry-can of water to carry. Sometimes they are told to attempt to maintain a patrol organisation, or to stay in a set group. These devices not only give the candidates some purpose, but make their final capture a near certainty. Even so, the hunters, which may include search parties from other regiments, play cat and mouse with the victims for several days and nights. Much of the action actually happens in the dark, when the hunters deploy lights as well as dogs. As Mack remembered:

'We were dropped somewhere in the Black Mountains. I still don't know where to this day. It was dark. We were challenged while walking up a fire break in the woods on the first night by the hunter force who were out looking for us. We took off and managed to escape… But of course you know you are going to get caught. You start off being dropped in a corridor 40 to 50 kilometres wide and it narrows to half a kilometre. If you go over the line – across the border, so to speak – you're out of bounds and you've failed.'

Andy McNab's group did their best to hide in the

Top, An MP5, used by the SAS in hostage rescue situations. **Bottom**, An Ingram sub-machine gun. **Defence Picture Library**

thickest bushes they could find during the day, thus avoiding the attentions of a company of the Guards and helicopters, who provided an Airborne Reaction hunter force. The escapers moved at night where possible, attempting to make contact with the Directing Staff, who played the part of friendly 'agents' for the purposes of the exercise. There was little opportunity to use his new-found skill in food scavenging, but at one point his team was handed a bin liner, which contained, of all things, raw tripe. After this, he risked approaching a farm house where the occupants gave him stew, tea, and Christmas cake. Like many participants, McNab was caught early on in the exercise; in such cases the prisoners are held for a few hours and then released again to continue.

INTERROGATION

However well the candidates have performed, they are rounded up for the final capture and the most controversial part of the exercise, the interrogation. Just how rough this is depends on the enthusiasm of the hunters and interrogators, who are themselves often under training, and how much bad publicity such courses have recently attracted. Sometimes there is the odd bruise or rough handling. Once in a while, as in an infamous incident when captives were thrown out of a stationary truck onto the road, a limb

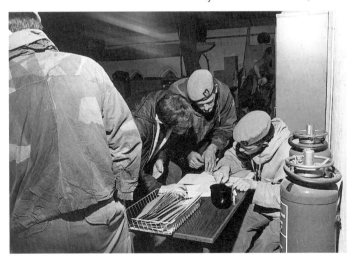

Though the eye of the press concentrates on the 'gung ho' aspects of the SAS, much of its work includes the patient gathering of intelligence which can be the making or breaking of an operation. Note the short SAS wind proof smocks in both camouflaged and plain material.

may be broken. For the most part, however, the interrogations are uncomfortable, threatening, psychological, and designed to trick, bamboozle or bore the victims into giving away more than their nam, rank and number.

The specific techniques are many and varied, and give the trainees just a taste of the possibilities they may face if captured for real. Sensory deprivation may include hoods, blindfolds, and long periods of silence, or white electronic noise. Being put in stress positions causes aching limbs; sleep deprivation may cause disorientation and chronic fatigue. Captives can be stripped naked, possibly hosed down with water, and then abused by male and female interrogators. Apparently more benign team members may adopt a bureaucratic regime, producing myriad official-looking forms and enticing the subjects to confirm or deny their contents, for the Red Cross or otherwise. Other pairs of questioners adopt 'nice and nasty' patterns of interrogation, bawling insults, then expressing concern and willingness to offer food, drink, and cigarettes. Sometimes the same questions are asked repeatedly in different ways to encourage a slip.

Some of the worst things the prisoners have to face are the unexpected, like threats of real violence which do not actually materialize. One party of prisoners was hooded and shackled to a disused railway line, within hearing of a moving train. Another year, a group was threatened with power tools held close to their heads. In another instance the interrogators put on an impressive, though totally fictional, beating in an adjoining room in which members of the team punched mattresses, screamed, and pretended to plead or vomit. On another occasion, a barking and apparently vicious dog was kept handy. One man was put in a room full of flashing lights without any explanation or questions. Army medical personnel are in attendance, but do not usually declare themselves unless the victims break down and give up the course.

The experience of Peter Crossland in 1986 was

harsh, but not untypical: 'The hunter force doesn't mess about when they capture you and somehow I ended up with a broken rib. No matter: once captured you are subjected to the regulation resistance to interrogation training. Hood on, stood in the stress position, feet spread with hands against the wall for hours. With a broken rib it was no joke. While all this was happening, they play what they call "white sound". It buzzes at you all the time, and is designed to wear you down or make you crack up. Every couple of hours or so, you get dragged off into an interrogation room. Here you are put in front of a trained interrogator – some prat who obviously gets off on seeing SAS candidates strip naked. Then he asks you loads of stupid questions.'

Sarah Ford, who worked on intelligence attached to the SAS, underwent a very similar experience a couple of years later, and was given few concessions on account of her sex: 'As I passed the corner of the outbuilding on my left, I saw the blur of black balaclavas and combat kit. Suddenly a group of four or five men roared onto the path and jumped on me… I landed with a thud on my back. One of them produced a rough Hessian sack, dragged it over my head and tied it securely around my neck… Having my sight removed was the worst part… I sensed I was being dragged down a long corridor… I was roughly pulled upright by a violent tug under the

Loading the Hercules C130 at night. Rapid deployment of men and stores is often the work of the RAF Special Forces Squadron, last known to be based at RAF Lyneham in Wiltshire.

armpits. My arms were yanked behind my back and held in two less than delicate arm locks… there was a horrendous disorientating crackling noise seeping from every direction, as if every inch of the walls was conducting the sound of a badly-tuned radio. Its pitch, frequency and volume were unwavering. There was nothing in the white noise to focus on, but it was just loud enough to drown out normal conversation and disrupt your thinking.' This was followed by the usual questions of the nice and nasty variety, more white noise, more stress positions with the odd whack on the back, and a strip search. Most of the SAS candidates make it through the evasion and interrogation, although even at this stage a few are 'Returned To Unit'.

SAS KIT

With the final test over, the successful candidates are now 'badged', receiving the coveted winged dagger. Usually the regimental beret is presented by the Commanding Officer in person. For many, this achievement of a long-term ambition is an uncharacteristically emotional moment. Soldier 'I' felt he had won 'the prize' and become part of the 'Praetorian Guard'. For Peter Crossland, it was a moment he would 'always remember'. Another man described himself as 'chuffed' and 'walking on air', in the same way as when his children were born.

The successful candidate is now permanently attached to a squadron, A, B, D, or G. Though there may be little difference in theory, G is so called because it is the Guards Squadron. Additionally, according to Mike Curtis, D is the traditional home of ex-Paratroopers, whilst B attracts many Australians, New Zealanders, and Fijians. A Squadron is the most laid-back, and sartorially challenged.

The SAS man is now entitled to certain official distinctions of dress. The beige beret and winged dagger badge are the most obvious, but there is also a blue regimental stable belt with regimental badge buckle. Sadly for those entitled to them, the beret and the belt are seldom seen outside the barracks and never on active service, for reasons of security. Very often, the SAS man will wear lightweight DPM combats, with or without the issue smock, or the 'Jersey Man's Heavy', or 'woolly pully' pullover, and will appear very much like any other soldier. Ordinary berets and helmets will be worn when the Regiment wishes to be inconspicuous against the military background. At times when this is unnecessary, there will be more evident individuality with camouflaged peaked caps, woollen skull caps, and jungle hats common choices. Ordinary army boots are worn, but many troopers purchase various types of their own. At one time, Danner boots with Gore-tex linings were particularly popular.

Opposite, **Soldier of 22nd Special Air Service Regiment, Iraq,1991. The central figure is a Trooper of D Squadron as he would have appeared after re-supply in the desert. The large Arab coat is of the type bought in Saudi Arabia and brought in by helicopter when it was realised that cold weather was hampering effectiveness. The coat is worn over belt kit and camouflage combats, with desert boots and** *shemag* **headgear. The thin leather aviator gloves provide some protection for the hands whilst retaining sufficient sensitivity and grip for the operation of the Armalite and M 203 grenade launcher.**

With the exception of the regimental winged dagger beret and cap badges in cloth and metal respectively, which were not worn in action, the other items are typical of those making

up the substantial loads carried by B Squadron road watch patrols in January 1991. At the top is the Belgian-designed Minimi 5.56 mm, a simple and robust light machine gun, weighing only 6.5 kg. It fires from a belt contained in a box magazine and is effective to about 800 metres. Its lightness and high rate of fire make it an ideal Special Forces arm. Below the Bergen, is the TACBE tactical beacon and radio. The prime use of this was to alert friendly aircraft to the presence of the SAS and to summon assistance. The Romanian made AKM assault rifle, seen bottom left, is a member of the Russian Kalashnikov family of weapons. It was one of several similar arms used by the Iraqis, though this type was notable for its forward pistol style grip.

SAS troopers would be expected to be familiar with and use captured Kalashnikovs.

At the bottom centre of the picture is the Browning semi-automatic pistol, with holster, lanyard, spare magazine and 9 mm ammunition. The Grenade Anti Personnel L2A2 is a high explosive grenade based on the US M 26 and weighs 395 gr. After the pin is withdrawn, the bomb is thrown releasing the lever. Once this is done, the fuse delay is between four and a half and five seconds before detonation. The main fragmentation effect is provided by a notched wire coil within the grenade that breaks up with the explosion. A method used by the SAS when grenades have to be carried long distance to the battlefield is to splay the pins further and tape down the handles

preventing accidents.

Bottom right is the single shot 66 mm Light Anti-Tank Weapon, M72, seen in both its closed travelling mode and open firing position. Sighted to 350 metres, the LAW is capable of penetrating about 305 mm of armour using a fin stabilised HEAT or high explosive anti-tank rocket. Just above the LAW, is the 'Elsie' anti personnel mine. The jerrycan with two sand bags for water, rations, ammunition and other small items are typical of the extra weight carried by members of the Bravo Two Zero patrol, underlining the old SAS dilemma of overload, or under equipment. The PCR 319 communications set was the main patrol radio, a significant burden for the patrol signaller, but a lifeline capable of 'burst transmissions' difficult for the enemy to intercept.
Painting by Richard Hook

Most soldiers are particular about the way they keep their equipment, but the SAS are more careful than most, with functionality paramount. Particularly important is the rucksack or Bergen, external square frame models often being preferred. In the 1990s, the 60-litre capacity Cyclops, and the 80-litre Crusader were both popular. Usually, the Bergen will remain packed ready for field service at short notice. In the bottom will be many of the regular items and spare clothing for use in the field: fleece jackets, waterproofs, DPM hooded jackets and T-shirts are all popular. In the top or in more accessible places will be smaller 'grab bags'. These are kept so that should it become necessary to jettison the main pack, the smaller bags can quickly be extracted. The grab bags will hold the really vital equipment, such as demolition stores, medical kit, or radio. With these tools of the trade and a belt kit, the patrol can continue to function.

The SAS man's clothing varies to match the climate in which he operates. In the jungle, clothing is light and the DPM tropical hat or a bandanna may be worn, but long sleeves and long trousers are usually retained on the basis that heat is more bearable than insect attack and the effects of the undergrowth. Tropical boots of rubber and canvas are worn, sometimes with the addition of metal plates to protect the feet against *'pungi'* stake booby traps. In the desert, brown and sand DPM combats are now the rule, and again long sleeves are preferred to help avoid sunburn. *Shemags* are used as a practical protection against sun and sand, and goggles are generally found more practical than sun glasses. In many deserts, the night can be surprisingly cold, as bitter experience in the Gulf and elsewhere has demonstrated, so pullovers, hollow fill 'Fitzroy' jackets, and aviator's gloves are often taken into such areas.

The Arctic has prompted the use of more special purpose clothing than virtually any other environment, and practical experience dating back to the Second World War has been put to good use. A layer approach is commonly adopted, often

starting with long sleeved, and legged cotton, 'long johns', and two pairs of socks, the pair nearest the skin being wool or wool blend. Over these foundations may be worn a selection of the following: Royal Marine DPM trousers with velcro fastenings, shirt, 'Fitzroy' jacket, fleece, Gore-tex smock, and white lightweight snow camouflage trousers, smock, and Bergen cover. Woolly hats, balaclavas, silk and cotton face masks, and goggles cover the head.

Mountain boots may be protected by Gore-tex gaiters. Ordinary British Army skis and bindings can be used, but Mountain Troop members in particular are likely to have their own private purchase skis and fittings. Snow shoes are preferred for conditions of deep loose snow. Commercial ski gloves are also sometimes used, but the approved system is two pairs of gloves, with a thin cotton pair next to the skin. Mittens may be worn, but have to be easily removable for the use of weapons and equipment. On some small arms, the removal of the trigger guard is possible allowing the use of bulky gloves, and such a procedure was indeed sanctioned in the official manual to the old Self Loading Rifle. Yet removing trigger guards can compromise both safety, and accurate shooting.

Just how much of the clothing is worn depends on the weather and tasks. Observation with little movement or access to hot food demands many layers and vigilance against frost bite. Rapid movement on skis in good weather is done in a minimum of clothing, with layers added when movement ceases. Sun burn is almost as much of a hazard as snow blindness, especially at high altitude or in clear weather. Clothing is kept as dry and clean as is practical since wet and dirt compromise thermal quality, air circulation and camouflage appearance.

SPECIALIST TRAINING

Though the recruits are now SAS men, training is far from over. It is a regimental maxim that a man is

Special Air Service Regiment beret badge.

Planning an exercise in
Wales, where the Black
Mountains and the Brecon
Beacons remain primary UK
training areas for 22 SAS.

SAS soldiers can volunteer for boat troop, supported by Marines from the 539 Asst. Squad.
Defence Picture Library

not at peak efficiency until three years after he has been badged. This is at least in part because each squadron is itself divided into troops, each with its own specialization which takes time to develop and practice to maintain. These four specialist troops are Mountain, Boat, Mobility, and Air.

In Mountain Troop, all aspects of mountaineering and winter warfare are taught. SAS men have climbed on most of the world's major ranges and since 1984 there have been fatalities on Mont Blanc and Everest. In Boat Troop, the main speciality is amphibious warfare and the men learn about landings, sailing, sea navigation, and assault craft. Air Troop are the specialists for all types of parachuting and air landing. Mobility Troop specializes in ground vehicles, Land Rovers, motorcycles, maintenance, off road driving and navigation.

Mack undertook Mobility training in Canada, where specially adapted all-terrain motorcycles were used up and down hills and across rivers. Back in the UK, he took part in an exercise in which hire cars, furniture vans, and motorbikes were used first to reconnoitre an RAF base, and then to attack it with thunder flashes, flare guns and dummy charges. The bikes were deployed direct from the back of one of the vans through holes in the perimeter fence. In Germany, an exercise was organized in which the Troop tracked, covertly followed, and then kidnapped an American officer who had volunteered to form part of the training. In the mid-1990s, Mobility training also included driving the Land Rover 110, Scorpion light tank, and Honda 350 Quad bike. Navigation skills included the use of the most modern satellite or 'Satnav' equipment, and more traditional methods using maps and the stars.

Some of the most dangerous training is done by Air Troop, who soon graduate from the pedestrian static line jumps of the selection course to free fall. Training jumps are undertaken at low level and into water. Descents are also made in a variety of climates and conditions, and recent venues include

Pau in the South of France and Oman. Gaz Hunter experienced a particularly nasty moment in a low altitude jump on a NATO exercise over Germany: 'We had been flying since midnight, on and off oxygen, up and down to the tail gate, ready to go each time and then being cancelled, bent double under an all-up weight of about 50 kg, made up of Bergen, weapons, belt kit and an extra pack… The aircraft dropped lower at every attempt so that from our original jump height of 6,000 metres we were down to 2,000. At four in the morning, physically and mentally drained, we jumped… he had put us out right over the middle of a small German town at very low altitude… I waited for the height finder (HF) to auto-release the parachute. It failed. No dramas, this had happened to me before. But I wasn't going to wait. I hit the parachute with my elbows, trying to smash it free, knowing this would set me spiralling… I found the handle, ripped it out, down and away, and waited. No canopy. Furiously, I rolled in the air and pulled at it again and again. I was at 700 metres, falling at terminal velocity. I twisted frantically… I went for my front reserve handle… It snapped me vertical with an almighty back-breaking jolt… All the extra kit and my Bergen were still bundled up on the back of my legs. This had to hit the ground before I did, or the huge weight would snap my ankles on landing…

SAS soldiers take part in hostage rescue training.
Defence Picture Library

At about 20 metres I tipped the Bergen off my boots. There was a massive tug as the line caught the weight and held. At that moment there was a huge flash in the sky. A brilliant arc of white-blue light shot out into the darkness, followed by fountains of yellow sparks. There was a weird fizzing sound. The air around me crackled and hissed, I smelt burning'. Hunter had landed across a power line. He was lucky to live, but there have been several fatalities.

A special form of parachute training is 'HALO' – High Altitude, Low Opening. At its most extreme, HALO may involve jumps from over 25,000 feet using oxygen, whilst carrying equipment and weapon. These very long drops with a late deployment of the parachute can be tactically useful, as they may help to keep an aircraft out of missile or radar range, or ground observation, and expose the jumper to the minimum of time dangling at the end of his chute. A variation on the theme is 'HAHO' – High Altitude, High Opening. This has the advantage that, if wind conditions are favourable, the jumper can leave the plane and then glide for several kilometres towards a target. Useful though they are, high altitude jumps have serious drawbacks. The parachutist may fall victim to frostbite, is more prone to tumbling in the air, or parachute snags which cannot be rectified. Steve Devereux described the sensation of a fully equipped HALO jump at night over France as being like 'lying face down on a huge beach ball, trying to balance yourself with an 80-pound sack of potatoes strapped to the back of your legs and a 10-pound yard broom shoved down one side of your body. And there was the effect of someone constantly spraying iced water in your face. I was trussed up like a Christmas turkey in a 120 mph wind!' Experiments in the 1990s also investigated the use of microlight aircraft for the insertion of troops.

Once the Troop specialization has been learned, the men may then receive some instruction to acquaint them with the rudiments of the other Troops' work. Men are also rotated through other Troops, keeping them fresh and giving them the widest possible experience. Within his own four-man patrol, each person will also have another skill to master as communications man, medic, linguist, or demolitions expert. Some of the skills are easier to practice realistically than others: demolitions men practice on trees and scrap vehicles, and also do a Home Made Explosves (HME) module; languages and communications are best taught in the field, preferably abroad.

The medics start with dummies, photos and theoretical tests but soon progress to the real thing. In the UK this may mean a stint as a Medical Assistant in a National Health Service hospital, helping to treat injured people under supervision. In the 1980s, Frank Collins recalled stitching faces, setting limbs, helping to administer anaesthesia, and being taught to recognize more tricky problems like blood on the lungs or head injuries. During Third World exercises, SAS medics often assist the local populations with basic medical problems. Bandaging, stitching, and administering drugs for common ailments is normal practice, but members of the Regiment have been known to deliver babies, even on active service. Communications may not be as physically arduous as it once was, since equipment is getting smaller, and often messages are relayed by 'burst transmission'. Nevertheless there is now a greater variety of equipment, and a basic morse proficiency of twelve words per minute is still required.

On top of all this, an effort is made to put SAS men of whatever Troop or specialization through the Counter Revolutionary Warfare Wing facility so that they may be useful in counter-terrorism. Usually this will mean upgrading sniper and assault skills for the urban environment, as well as learning about hostage rescue and the nuances of politically motivated crime. Sniper training comes first, and involves not only actual shooting and familiarity with the weapon, but learning adjustments for wind speed and air temperature. Code drills are also learned so that the sniper will know which part of a building he should be aiming at, in which 'red' may mean the right side of the building, whilst 'one, three' means first floor, three windows in from the side.

All being well, the trainees now graduate to actual assault training. In the 1990s, the Close Quarter Battle house was so arranged that its facilities represented a block of flats and two other buildings. Various approaches were practiced, from windows, doors, and perhaps most impressively of all, from helicopters on and off the roof. Standard kit for these activities is the black overalls, teamed with fire resistant masks, gloves, body armour, and respirators. The Heckler and Koch MP 5 is the main weapon with four 30-round magazines, but SIG Saur pistols, pyrotechnics and door charges are also used. Radios with throat microphones are preferred for ease of communication without letting go of the weapon or rope.

Special missions or particular postings may also involve additional training, such as jungle or mountain refreshers, or anti-tank or missile work. Even Northern Ireland may require extra training. At one time, those expected to drive undercover in the province were given advanced or speed driving courses by the Police, including such exotics as pursuit drives and hand-brake turns. Every soldier in the British Army receives training, but clearly the SAS have more training, in greater variety, than any other unit.

All SAS troops must pass the basic parachute course.
Defence Picture Library

SAS IN ACTION

On 30 April 1980, international terrorism came to London. That day, six Arabs from Khuzestan, sponsored by Iraq, seized the Iranian Embassy in Princes Gate. As they burst in, PC Trevor Lock of the Diplomatic Protection Group attempted to prevent them forcing the inner doors, but shots were fired and the police officer was himself grabbed and added to those 25 persons still inside who became hostages. Three people managed to escape from the back of the building in the confusion and raised the alarm, though Dr Ali Afrouz, the *chargé d'affaires*, was injured jumping from a window and captured by the terrorists. For six days, there was stalemate. Police negotiators attempted to bring about a peaceful resolution, whilst those inside the embassy made various demands, including the release of Arab prisoners from Iranian jails, and a bus to take the kidnappers and some of the hostages to the airport. The demands were backed with threats of violence.

THE KILLING HOUSE

Unknown to the terrorists, their appearance in London was an absolute gift to the SAS. Since 1972, when the Black September group had kidnapped Israeli athletes at the Munich Olympics and a rescue attempt had ended in a blood-bath, successive governments had been only too aware how vulnerable Britain might be to acts of terrorism. In those years of relative peace, the Regiment had been tasked with the establishment of a Counter Revolutionary Warfare wing to deal with just such an eventuality. The wing was given a full-time staff of 20.

A key ingredient of the preparations was the evolution of realistic Close Quarter Battle and bodyguard training, and the establishment of the Killing House at Stirling Lines, Hereford. Initially, the Killing House had been a relatively simple affair, not unlike the 'French Village' or 'Hogan's Alley' concepts, pioneered at Camp Perry in the

US just after the First World War. In these, trainee practical shooters had been placed in a more or less realistic combat or policing environment and suddenly shown a series of targets, friendly or hostile, and told to engage them. The challenge was not only to fire accurately, but quickly, and to hit the right target. The Killing House was started with a single room with a few paper targets into which the troopers had to burst, and with strictly limited time, take out the cardboard opposition. By the end of the 1970s, there were six rooms, allowing the use of more complicated scenarios, and interiors which represented everything from domestic situations to aircraft and power stations. The walls of the rooms were so lined as to limit the possibility of ricochets, and the men often formed sub-sections or combat groups armed with a variety of weapons. Paper targets had been replaced by more realistic dummies. Despite accidents, there were also experiments with the use of 'live' hostages.

The Regiment responded keenly to the Princes Gate situation, key members being alerted by pagers, and reporting to their 'Toads' or Assault Team leaders. The first 24 men of B Squadron were soon on their way, travelling in plain clothes in a mixture of furniture vans and Range Rovers. As was laid out in the Standard Operating Procedure, the Regiment went prepared with a ready-made plan for Immediate Action, and then, having evaluated the position, began to evolve a more subtle and detailed scheme called the Deliberate Assault Plan. In practice, this meant that had violence broken out immediately, the troopers would have gone straight for the front door, broken in, smashed windows, thrown in CS gas, and engaged the terrorists in a fire fight. Fortunately, the negotiations provided a vital delay and a bloody battle was avoided. Negotiations continued for several days and some of the captives, including sick BBC employee Chris Cramer, were released. One of the first break-throughs for the security

forces was the discovery that it had been the embassy caretaker's day off when the hostages were taken. He was thus at liberty, and able to give detailed intelligence regarding the building. Critically, he was able to let the authorities know that not only were there security doors, but that the windows to the ground and first floors were armoured. He also worked on detailed plans of the interiors, from which it was possible for Royal Engineers to build a model of wood and hessian on which the Regiment could plan its attack. Further detail was filled in by released hostages. The emerging task was undoubtedly monumental: the embassy was on six floors, had fields of fire to the front and rear, and was a warren of 50 rooms. Two of the terrorists, including their leader Ali Mohammed code name 'Salim', were believed to have Skorpion sub-machine guns, while the others had pistols, grenades and possibly explosives. On the plus side, it appeared feasible to get men close to one or more of the windows or skylights without detection, since there were insufficient terrorists to cover all eventualities. On the minus side, it might take time to locate all the hostages, time which the enemy might use to start killing.

Further data was provided by a variety of active means. Snipers were positioned on vantage points and reported movements, while attempts were

made by MI5 to insinuate cameras and microphones into chimneys and walls. Noise of tapping and drilling would have compromised these efforts, so louder noise was created as a camouflage. The Gas Board dug up nearby streets with pneumatic drills and flight paths were subtly altered to bring jets closer.

Perhaps the most dangerous exercise was the rooftop reconnaissance undertaken by a three-man SAS team. As a Trooper nicknamed 'Snapper' recorded: 'It was about eleven when we climbed through the skylight of Number 16 and on to the roof. It was a fine night. The stars were out. It was Bank Holiday weekend so the streets were empty, which made it really eerie. We made our way as quietly as possible about 30 yards across the slates between thickets of aerials, like cat burglars. There was silence apart from the creaking of our belt kit, the rustle of our clothing and the scuffing sound of our running shoes. Suddenly there was a crack like a pistol going off. We froze. Roy pointed to his foot. He'd broken a slate. We looked across at the sniper hidden on the roof of Number 14, gave him the thumbs up and carried on. Then Roy stopped and I went up to him. He was pulling at a skylight, but it was locked solid. Pete suggested peeling back the lead waterproofing. Fifteen minutes later he'd done it. He lifted out the glass panel, unlocked it and opened the skylight. We could see in the moonlight that we were above a small bathroom and I got a dose of adrenaline… We'd found what we were looking for – a guaranteed entry point.'

On the basis of the new information, the Deliberate Action Plan 'Operation Nimrod' was evolved. The Immediate Action unit was superseded by a larger group, split into two Teams, 'Red' and 'Blue'. Red would deal with the top half of the building, Blue would deal with the basement, ground, and first floors. The teeth of Red Team were four sub-sections of four men: two of these sub-sections were detailed to abseil

SAS on the roof at Princes Gate, May 1980. Body armour, Heckler and Koch SMGs, and respirators are in evidence.

from the roof to the back balcony on the second storey, whilst a third attacked the third storey by means of ladders. The remaining four men of Red Team would blow in the skylight and enter direct from the roof. Blue Team's attack included assault both on ground and first floor level, and men with framed charges intended to deal with the armoured glass windows. As the then Director of the SAS Brigadier Peter de la Billière put it, the essence of the plan was: 'to attack every floor of the building simultaneously, and break in so fast on all levels that the gunmen would not have time to execute anyone. Success depended on every SAS man knowing his task precisely… to pick out the terrorist, recognise every hostage, and keep within pre-set boundaries so there was no risk of shooting each other.'

By 5 May, the siege had entered a new and dangerous phase. There was reason to believe that one hostage had been killed that morning, and if any more died, the police agreed that control should be handed over to the SAS. Just after five, PC Lock managed to use a telephone and warn the outside world that the terrorists were barricading themselves in and threatening to kill all the hostages. At six, the Home Secretary William Whitelaw convened a meeting which agreed the circumstances under which the 'DAP' would be put into action. As 'Snapper', waiting in the forward holding area, put it: 'We lay on our camp beds, wondering what would happen. I was wearing my black overalls, belt kit and lightweight boots. The MP 5, body armour, respirator and assault waistcoat loaded with stun grenades were close to hand if the word came to go. I stripped and cleaned my weapons, hoping that this wouldn't go on and on. Waiting around was boring. Your mind is active all the time.'

There was not long to wait. Within minutes of the Home Secretary's deliberations, more shots rang out, and the body of the hostage who had been killed earlier in the day was flung out onto the pavement. The Prime Minister, Margaret Thatcher, gave her permission for the use of the SAS, and just after 7pm the police handed over control to Lieutenant Colonel Michael Rose.

BREAK IN

At 7.25, the signal 'London Bridge' was given. Seconds later, there was a loud explosion and a shattering of glass: Red Team had blown in the skylight, abseilers dropped from the roof, and Blue Team sprang into action lower down. Stun grenades and CS gas were put in to disorientate and subdue the opposition.

Red Team rapidly smashed their way in and found most of the opposition on the second floor. Here there was a three-way tussle in the office where one of the terrorists was fighting off PC Lock: an SAS man intervened to fire a long burst. Shots from the telex room and a running man alerted the soldiers to the fact that the hostages

On a balcony of the Iranian Embassy preparing to enter. A Heckler and Koch MP 5 with telescopic stock and light mounted over the barrel may be seen slung from the man in the centre.

A hostage makes his escape
from Princes Gate as fire
breaks out. An SAS man
appears in a window recess.

were being killed and they rushed in. One soldier managed to identify a terrorist immediately and 'blew his brains all over the place' with a shot from his Browning. A second was similarly accounted for, before the hostages surged out of the door, some with raised hands, others screaming.

'Mack' was a soldier of Blue Team tasked to attack at first floor level: 'Once I found my footing on the target balcony, I began to place the charge. There was a *zing* and a puff of dust at my feet and I realized that I had an incoming shot from somewhere… Then there was a clunk beside me and I looked down to see a grenade rolling off the balcony. Then it was gone, so it didn't bother me. The terrorist who had dropped it had forgotten to take out the pin… As soon I had placed the charge, we took off back across onto the other balcony, shouting "fire" as we went. This was the signal to the guys to detonate the charge. All this happened in seconds… The balustrade was blown clean off… we stepped through the rubble and smoke into the room and went into our rehearsed routine.'

Whilst Mack secured BBC man Sim Harris, two of his colleagues rushed on to confront Salim. In the confusion, one of the terrorists pushed past into a room which had already been cleared, firing as he went. Mack and others followed this man and found him on a couch 'shot up all one side': he was finished off with a burst of fire. Stress, shock, and a whiff of gas, when his respirator had been knocked, made Mack vomit into his mask.

Meanwhile Snapper had been with the group from Blue Team, which had been tasked to blow in the French windows and clear the basement. To his horror, he could see that one of the abseilers was stuck just above the vital spot, swinging dangerously on his rope, enveloped in smoke where grenades had set light to the curtains. The men smashed the windows with a sledge hammer rather than blow up their colleague. Descending to the basement, they kicked in doors, threw in stun grenades, shot off locks,

and inadvertently sprayed a dustbin with fire.

Coming up to the ground floor reception, they met the gaggle of hostages being herded out by members of Red Team. Someone shouted that there was a terrorist taking cover amongst the civilians. 'I couldn't fire… the bullets would have gone through him and into my mates. So I clubbed him on the back of the neck with the MP5 as hard as I could and down he went. Rusty pushed him and he rolled down the stairs'. He was then riddled with 22 rounds from close range before he could activate his grenade. Snipers in Hyde Park claimed to have hit a terrorist trying to escape from a balcony. The last terrorist, Fowzi Bavadi Nejad, was captured alive.

Subsequent checks identified Salim lying dead on the first floor balcony; two terrorists dead in the telex room; one in the office; and one in the hallway by the front door. One of the hostages had been killed, another injured. The SAS had no fatalities but the unfortunate abseiler, Corporal Tommy Palmer, was quite badly burned, and another man grazed by a bullet. The assault had taken just 12 minutes. The SAS were thanked immediately by the Home Secretary and Prime Minister, and Palmer received the Military Medal, one of five men decorated.

The Iranian Embassy siege thrust the Regiment back into public consciousness and gained it many plaudits. Yet public awareness has proved to be a double-edged sword: the Regiment is extremely unlikely to suffer amalgamation or disbandment, and has become generally popular with the public, but it is feared that with so much now known about the SAS, clandestine operations could be compromised, or an enemy alerted.

NORTHERN IRELAND

The SAS were first deployed in Northern Ireland in 1969, though by all accounts this foray was of short duration and limited impact. In one celebrated instance, men actually appeared in public in uniform. This may have been useful in publicity terms, but was a disaster as a prelude to any undercover operation. The Regiment came back, in small patrol-sized groups, attempting to stop gun running across the border in 1970-1972. During 1971 alone, approximately 170 people died in 'the Troubles', a figure roughly evenly divided between terrorists, security forces, and civilians.

It has been claimed that the particularly large numbers of terrorists killed in the early days of 'the Troubles' were a result not so much of the relative inexperience of the IRA at this period, as of a willingness by the SAS to 'shoot on sight'. Paul Bruce claims that he, as a serving SAS man, was instructed to carry out contract-style killings of IRA men during this period. Bruce's claims repeat, somewhat inaccurately, many of the allegations made in Captain Fred Holroyd's *War Without Honour*.

If the SAS ever were ordered to carry out killings, it has certainly been the exception to the rule. The vast majority of SAS memoirs dealing with Northern Ireland speak of frustrating hours of surveillance, of seeing known suspects, and of being ordered not to shoot unless they, or others, are in immediate danger. Many SAS men speak of what they would have liked to have done, and were never allowed to. As Harry McCallion put it: 'The SAS has no *carte blanche* to kill in Ulster; like any soldier on duty in the Province they are governed by rules of engagement, the "yellow card" rules. However, the SAS comprises highly trained, extremely aggressive soldiers, and putting them near armed IRA terrorists is a little like putting hungry wolves near to red meat.' Soldier 'I' felt this as a 'new and dangerous frustration' of 'not being able to get to grips with the enemy'.

Whilst carrying out their dangerous and often thankless tasks, SAS men have to live *incognito*, often in Portakabins within security bases, surrounded by corrugated iron walls, concrete sentry boxes, and netting designed to frustrate rocket-propelled grenades. It can be, as Soldier 'I' observed, a 'cold grey world', both 'squalid' and 'claustrophobic'. Decision making in the pressurized environment of Northern Ireland is extremely hazardous: armed terrorists, passers by, informers, and even other security services are difficult to distinguish.

Patience is arguably the greatest virtue required of the SAS man in Northern Ireland. Harry McCallion's account of surveillance is typical of many: 'My location was a small wood next to a suspected target's house. For the next four weeks, we were sleeping in two-hour shifts, eating cold food, unable to move in the daylight hours and urinating and defecating into plastic bags stored in

our Bergens for removal… Lying for hours on end is an art form. If you are not careful, your legs become like dead weights and the urge to move them is overwhelming. To stop this most of us had little routines. Starting with one leg, we would concentrate on moving our toes, then the foot inside the boot, then slowly flexing each muscle of the leg… In this way you helped to prevent both "dead leg" and cramp. Cramp was a particular hazard as it could literally cost you your life. We used to rotate watches so that nobody spent more than an hour actually watching a target… At night we would use our peripheral vision to watch an object.'

In the field, camouflage and stalking skills are at a premium. In built-up areas, other ways are practiced to blend in. Sometimes the Regiment appear as ordinary civilians, manual labourers, men hanging about in pubs wearing denim, council workers, or van drivers, but disguising anything but a very small number of very fit, non-Irish men of military age can be difficult, whatever the length of their hair. Pairing them with female soldiers, or creating an artificial job like a broken-down vehicle or a street repair can help. One man recorded being hidden inside a cardboard box in a factory, a cover which was quickly blown by the kindly inquiries of the manager as to his well being. Sometimes SAS patrols are blended with ordinary Army or RUC patrols, and dropped off along the route. Wearing the uniform or equipment of other units is commonplace. Berets are changed for those of the signallers or infantry, Armalites for ordinary SA 80 infantry rifles.

The Regiment may indeed have killed more terrorists than any other unit, but the prime reason seems to be that the unit is the weapon of choice when opportunity arises to frustrate terrorism. If knowledge of an assassination attempt is disclosed, it is often the SAS who are chosen to lay in wait for the killers; when an arms cache is discovered, it is often the SAS who will stake out the area; when covert work is required, it is often the SAS who go undercover. It is therefore remarkable that the Regiment has lost only four men in the province, and two of these died in car accidents. None were killed prior to 1978: strong circumstantial evidence of the relative level of regimental involvement, and of its professionalism. The Regiment has killed more than 30 terrorists, the majority of them armed at the time of contact. They have also arrested many more than they have killed. Even so there have been a few spectacular own goals: as when two men of B Squadron were arrested for attempted bank robbery in Londonderry, or when John Boyle, a curious but innocent youth, was shot dead when examining an arms cache.

In 1974, a new unit called 14 Intelligence Company was set up in the murderous 'bandit country' of Armagh, specifically to gather intelligence, under the leadership of Captain Julian Ball. The outfit used various cover names, including 4 Field Survey Troop, but already had strong SAS connections since Ball was previously an SAS ranker, and would subsequently serve with the Regiment as an officer. In any case, unexpectedly vigorous, and not always subtle, activity was the result. One senior IRA man was actually snatched from south of the border and delivered to the authorities in the north, two more were shot. Fire was being fought with fire. From 1972 to 1976, there were more than 200 deaths each year, most of them civilians killed by both Republican and Loyalist paramilitaries.

In the meantime, the somewhat risky political decision had been taken for the formal reintroduction of the SAS to the province, a fact which was announced in early 1976. Initially whole squadrons were deployed, later a smaller job specific 'Ulster Troop' was established. Early successes included the arrest of two IRA officers, and the ambush and killing of an armed and hooded IRA man. Against this had to be set the farce of two covert SAS 'Q' cars which strayed south of the border and were detained by the Garda. Over the next year or two, several men were shot whilst visiting IRA weapons stores and some of these were put down to ambush teams of the Regiment. During the controversial Ballysillan incident, an IRA active service unit was ambushed planting a bomb; unfortunately a passerby was killed as well as terrorists.

TERRORIST TARGETS

Perhaps the most appalling incident during the SAS involvement in Northern Ireland was the murder of Captain Robert Nairac in May 1977, although strictly speaking, Nairac was not an SAS officer, but a Grenadier Guards officer attached as Special Branch Liaison to A Squadron. Nairac was an Oxford graduate, who appeared to possess an odd mixture of intelligence, perception, and naivety. His work in the province included a thoughtful report entitled *Talking to People in South Armagh*, which proposed a 'hearts and minds' approach, by which the flow of youthful recruits to the IRA might be cut off. Unfortunately Nairac was prone to take risks when undercover, and had a dangerous propensity to mix uniform and plain clothes work, thereby making himself a more obvious target.

On 14 May, Nairac left Bessbrook to meet a potential contact at the Three Steps, Drumintee.

Though he had been offered back-up by the SAS Operations Officer, Captain David Collet, he preferred instead to trust to his own resources and a shoulder-holstered 9mm Browning, which had been slightly modified for ease of concealed use by a reduction of the butt, and an oversized safety catch. In the event, Nairac's cover was quickly seen through, and he was lured outside the bar and set upon by two, and soon four, assailants. It seems that Nairac did not immediately draw his weapon. Severely beaten, he was driven away south of the border where IRA hit man Liam Townson was called out of another bar to perform a cold-blooded execution. According to the *Daily Telegraph* account, quoting Republican sources, the dead man's body was destroyed in a meat processing factory.

The similarities of Nairac's end with the murder of two Signals corporals later on suggests very real lessons for security forces faced with capture. Most specifically that either hesitancy, or over confidence, are potentially fatal, and that running away, or shooting, are better options, as the first contacted protagonists seldom have the will, or the sudden decision-making capability, to carry out murder. SAS men surprised in their vehicles have succeeded in making off on a number of occasions. One novice group of three got out and ran when cornered, and lived, despite the humiliation of losing a vehicle and at least one weapon. Others have shot first, though there have been questions to answer afterwards.

The Regiment's first badged fatality in action against the IRA was Captain Richard Westmacott in 1980. A tip-off had been received that the IRA had obtained a US M60 machine gun and were preparing an ambush on Antrim Road, Belfast. The SAS responded, inadvertently launching the storming of the wrong house. At this point, the M60 opened up from nearby, firing a couple of bursts, and killing Captain Westmacott. Despite the initial bungle, and losing their officer, the SAS now surrounded the right house and the enemy were forced to surrender.

A number of successes were achieved over the next few years without further loss to the Regiment. In January 1981, they were instrumental in interrupting a Loyalist attack, making arrests, and perhaps bizarrely helping to save the life of Republican activist Bernadette Devlin. Late in 1983, an arms cache was located in which weapons already used in terrorist attacks were stored. Two IRA men were ambushed and killed as they pulled out an Armalite rifle. In July 1984, four IRA men were surprised taking incendiary bombs into a factory. One man, who was also carrying two pistols,

The regulation SAS headstone with winged dagger badge and motto. Having formerly served as a signaller, 'Dave' Naden passed selection in 1969 and went on to serve in Dhofar and Northern Ireland. He was killed in a road accident in Northern Ireland in 1978. Since the Falklands, parachute, road, mountaineering, and other accidents have actually outnumbered losses in combat.

was shot dead. Two were captured and arrested, though one man escaped.

The Regiment's second fatality came one night in December 1984 when SAS men travelling in Q cars obtained information about a potential bomb attack in Fermanagh. A pair of SAS men alighted from their car to question some suspicious-looking men near a van, and shooting started. Lance Corporal Alistair Slater let off a flare to illuminate the scene, and in doing so was hit. The regimental journal records that, though wounded, Slater attempted to return fire; he was awarded a posthumous Military Medal. As Frank Collins, a personal friend of Slater, recorded: 'The fleeing Provo halted to save his life and was being searched when Al's body was discovered. The terrorist then took advantage of the situation and tried to escape, again drawing his pistol. The rules say that in this situation you can shoot, and he was shot dead. Despite the security cordon the other terrorists managed to escape but one was killed in the process. He drowned trying to swim the river... The other two hit men were picked up by the police the next day, suffering from exposure.'

Perhaps the single biggest *coup* against IRA terrorists was the foiling of the attack on Loughgall police station on 8 May 1987. Intelligence had been gleaned that a group of IRA volunteers were going to smash their way into the station, preceded by a bomb-laden JCB. Ulster Troop, backed by reinforcements from G Squadron and local security forces, prepared a reception, concealing men and machine guns in and around the police station, and cut-offs on likely approach roads. As expected, the IRA gang led by Jim Lynagh crashed the earth mover through the station fence at the same moment as armed men jumped from a Toyota van and began to fire. At this cue, the SAS opened up with overwhelming fire power. Three IRA men died inside the van, two more behind it, and one standing by the driver's door. Two more began to run but were cut down as they reached the blocking parties. Nevertheless, the JCB bomb exploded, injuring three members of the security forces, and an innocent bystander was also caught in the crossfire and killed. The dead terrorists had pedigrees of IRA service stretching back many years: Lynagh, a former Sinn Fein councillor had served jail terms on both sides of the border for weapons and explosives convictions; Padraig McKearney was a Maze Prison escaper who had served various terms for possession of weapons. Several of the others already had minor convictions, and were admitted by Republican sources to have been long-term members of the movement.

Though not actually carried out in Northern Ireland, Operation Flavius of March 1988 was one of the most controversial SAS actions against terrorism. Intelligence was received that the IRA intended to detonate a bomb in Gibraltar, most likely aimed at a guard changing ceremony at which both servicemen and civilians would be present, and the SAS were called in to foil the plot. A team of about a dozen, together with M15 operatives, was moved in. It was believed, correctly, that the suspects had a large car bomb, and that this was going to be driven across the Spanish border, then remotely detonated. Ideally the suspects should be caught on Gibraltar with evidence of their intention, but not allowed to carry out the bombing. On Sunday 6 March, the three suspects were seen near a white Renault thought to contain a bomb, then walked away.

What exactly happened next has been a matter of argument ever since. It may be the case that the SAS team was caught on the hop: if the terrorists melted away there was every possibility that the Renault, or another vehicle might be detonated and cause massive loss of innocent life. Quick action was required, but how to stop possibly armed IRA operatives in busy streets without one or another detonating the bomb was no easy matter. In the event, one of the terrorists literally bumped into soldier 'A', who drew his Browning

pistol and challenged the man to stop. He kept going. The second male suspect had already begun to walk off in a different direction, possibly realizing arrest was imminent, and it looked as though one or more might make their escape. Soldier 'A' opened fire, and 'B', who had heard his 'garbled shout', joined in the fusillade. About a hundred yards away, the third person was challenged as the sound of shooting filled the air. Whether he intended surrender or not is unclear. Those confronting him say that a woman got between them and the target, then soldier 'D' got a clear view, and emptied nine rounds into him.

All three terrorists were now dead or dying on the street, having taken 27 bullets between them. This very public shooting caused a furore. On one side of the coin, it may have been that at the last moment one or more of the suspects attempted to give themselves up. On the other, a real car bomb was indeed discovered, though this was not the white Renault, and the actions of the persons challenged were not easy to interpret. That the IRA team had intended indiscriminate murder is difficult to deny. The dead were Mairead Farrell, who had served 10 years for a bombing in Northern Ireland; Danny McCann, who had a previous conviction for possession, and Sean Savage. All had been making use of one or

Damaged Pucara aircraft in the Falklands, 1982, a target for SAS raids.

more assumed identities in the last few days.

Between the 'Death on the Rock' and the latest ceasefire, the fight against terrorism has been continued. In August 1988, the SAS were involved in a sting which involved replacing a terrorist target with their own man, then ambushing the assassins. The IRA men fired first, but all three were killed. Two more assassins met similar fates in 1990 whilst creeping up on, or firing into UDR reservists' homes. In 1992, four more IRA men were killed just after perpetrating an attack on Coalisland police station, using a heavy machine gun.

COUNTER INVASION

With the Argentinian invasion of the Falkland Islands and South Georgia in April 1982, the history of the SAS moved into uncharted waters. Since the Second World War, the Regiment had been acting principally as a support to friendly regimes in the Third World and former Empire, and training for a NATO war in Europe, or to counter terrorism. The conflict with Argentina was none of these things. Independent British amphibious operations, on contested landing grounds, against an enemy equipped with the latest missiles was not the eventuality that either the Army or the SAS was expecting. No contingency plan existed for counter

invasion of the Falklands, and the role of the SAS had to evolve with circumstance. Nevertheless, Lieutenant Colonel Michael Rose, Commanding Officer of 22 SAS, was quick to signal the unit's readiness to assist any new Task Force.

The very day after the Argentine attack, 66 men of D Squadron, plus 14 signallers, commanded by Major Cedric Delves, were being assembled to participate. They were soon ordered by air to Ascension Island. Lieutenant Colonel Rose himself boarded the *Fearless*, with a team from headquarters and 200 tons of supplies. So it was that the Regiment was available for the first significant offensive action of the campaign, the recapture of South Georgia.

When the daring, if not suicidal, outline of Operation Paraquet (humorously known as 'Paraquat') reached the Task Force, the recipients were incredulous. The Regiment was to be in the forefront of a landing, with inadequate air cover, against an enemy superior in numbers ensconced on an inhospitable Antarctic Island. It is said that the Northwood Headquarters received the signal 'Kill off Paraquat before it kills us' in response to its order. Yet for this endeavour, the Mountain or number '19' Troop of D Squadron was to be in good company, being teamed with M Company of 42 Royal Marine Commando, and a few men of the Special Boat Squadron. The SAS troop of

The final Argentine surrender at Pebble Island, 1982. British troops supervise the movement of captured stores.

16 men, under experienced mountaineer Captain G.J. Hamilton, was to be landed by helicopter on the Fortuna Glacier, and from here they would climb down to find suitable landing beaches and put nearby settlements under observation.

On 21 April, the Wessex helicopters attempted to put Hamilton's troop ashore under howling wind and 'white-out' conditions. After two failures, they succeeded, but the problems had only just begun, for it took the SAS party several hours hauling their sledges to cover less than a mile. They had no option but to take shelter, though one of their tents was rapidly whipped away by the sub-zero wind. What had been an advance was about to change into a desperate rescue mission as the team now requested to be lifted out again. Of three helicopters sent to collect Hamilton's group, two crashed on their return journey, and tipped over onto the ice. Miraculously, there was only one minor casualty, Corporal Paul Bunker SAS. There now remained only one helicopter, a Mk 3 Wessex nicknamed 'Humphrey' piloted by Lieutenant Commander Stanley, to complete the evacuation.

With this ticklish job complete, a new plan had to be adopted. This time D Squadron's Boat, or '17' Troop, were given the task and took a more direct approach attempting a landing from Gemini inflatables which had been launched from

HMS Antrim. Yet this itself was not without significant risk, for three of the inflatables were suffering from engine problems, and once at sea the little flotilla was lashed by 100 mph gusts of wind blowing down off the ice. The result was that two boats drifted away; one was lucky to be saved by the irrepressible Humphrey. The other was driven ashore at Cape Saunders where the crew lay low in freezing conditions for three days until they felt it was safe to announce their position. The remaining three vessels made landfall on Grass Island to set up observation posts.

Following the masterful attack by Humphrey and two other helicopters on the Argentinian submarine *Sante Fe* on 25 April, it was decided that the time was ripe to go over to the offensive. Even so, given the lack of men and transport, it proved possible to put only 75 soldiers and Marines into the assault on Grytviken. The SAS contribution was two troops commanded by Major Delves, landed by helicopter at Hestesletten and then attacking on foot. The result was almost instant success, for the Argentinians were thoroughly demoralised by naval gunfire timed to coincide with the attack. In the event, the SAS men opened fire only twice, once to put a Milan missile into a suspicious-looking metal plate, and once against some seals whose surprise appearance

Next page, D Squadron Mountain Troop raid Argentine airfield on Pebble Island, 14-15 May, 1982. The Pebble Island raid by D Squadron was one of the most successful SAS actions of the Falklands campaign, disabling about a quarter of the Argentine aircraft on the Islands at a single stroke, with no fatalities amongst the attackers. Though three troops were ferried in by helicopter, only Captain G.J. Hamilton's Mountain Troop was committed to the climactic half-hour close assault of the airstrip.

The reconstruction shows several episodes during the assault. Delays to the commencement of the operation meant that time before dawn was short, so the action was brisk and violent, beginning at 7 am. A supporting bombardment was

called down from *HMS Glamorgan* by Captain Chris Brown, Royal Artillery, whilst the SAS 81 mm mortar team dropped illuminating rounds on the positions of the 3rd Marines who formed the enemy garrison. In this way, the Argentinians were shaken and lit up, whilst making it difficult for the defenders to identify the attackers. Under cover of the supporting fire, the SAS men came up to the perimeter in pairs, advancing by fire and movement. They then 'brassed up' the field with small arms fire, receiving a few shots in return from a bunker on the edge of the field. This was given heavy return fire.

The illustration shows troopers, foreground right, engaging the enemy position with a light machine gun, Armalite, and self loading rifles. The large

back blast is created by the discharge of a 66 mm rocket from a light anti-tank weapon, which the raiders used as a form of man portable artillery. The men wear a mixture of ordinary issue and private purchase DPM combat clothing and Gore-Tex jackets. According to one account, the first delivery of these jackets to the Regiment lost their water repellent qualities when a storeman mistakenly washed them at high temperature. Woollen caps, belt kit, and spare belts of ammunition are also in evidence. Bergens were not worn for the actual attack. Centre foreground, a slightly wounded man is given medical assistance by Staff Sergeant Philip Currass, a former member of the Royal Army Medical Corps, and holder of the Queens Gallantry Medal.

In the distance, beyond the burning Pucara aircraft, may be seen men moving up onto the strip to tackle planes at close quarters. A number were blown up with charges, but one defied the attackers and Trooper Raymond 'Pucara Paddy' Armstrong (a former Royal Green Jacket) can be seen climbing on board to disable it. Captain Hamilton is standing nearby, just about to give the word to fall back. Hamilton had commanded 19 (Mountain) Troop for just over a year before the Falklands and would receive a posthumous Military Cross for his part in the campaign. A total of 11 aircraft were accounted for during the raid, four Turbo-Mentors and a Skyvan, in addition to the Pucara ground attack planes.
Painting by Richard Hook.

was mistaken for enemy troops. Hamilton arrived at Grytviken and accepted the Argentinian surrender just ahead of the arrival of a Royal Marine battle group. Squadron Sergeant Major Gallagher ran up the Union flag. The recapture of South Georgia had been tough, but almost bloodless. Margaret Thatcher told the British public to 'Rejoice!', though there was much yet to be done.

ASSAULT AT PEBBLE ISLAND

Operation Prelim, the devastating SAS raid on Pebble Island off West Falkland on 15 May, marked a welcome return to the Regiment's original *forte* – unexpected and daring assault

against enemy air power. Stealthy though perilous reconnaissance by two four-man patrols from D Squadron's Boat Troop had ascertained that about a squadron of Argentine aircraft were present on the Pebble Island airstrip, and though they were guarded, the enemy sentries were not very vigilant. These findings were transmitted back to the *Hermes* on 13 May and the decision was made to take swift advantage.

The plan was that three troops led by Major Delves, totalling 45 men, would be ferried in by helicopter under cover of darkness, and march the final four miles to their destination. Whilst one troop provided a reserve, and another sealed the

Helicopter transport, a rare luxury during the Falklands campaign.

approaches to the nearby settlement, Captain Hamilton's Mountain Troop would attack the airstrip. Covering fire would be provided by *HMS Glamorgan*, and a mortar team which would have local defence given by a few men of Boat Troop. Time was a vital factor since if the raiders dallied, *Hermes* and other vessels supporting the operation might find themselves static by daylight, under observation, and vulnerable to attack.

Delays in deployment cut the time available to Hamilton's Troop on the target to a mere 30 minutes, and speed of movement on the ground was not helped by the fact that each man had to carry two bombs for the 81 mm mortar, and many had extra ammunition for the machine guns. The result was that the attack went in after only a minimum of preparation, as was described by an SAS man subsequently identified as 'David': 'The attack opened with a naval bombardment on to the feature directly overlooking the settlement. Then our own mortar opened up, lighting the whole place like it was bright daylight. The mortar was having a lot of trouble. Every time he fired the bloody thing, the whack of the pipe was kicking the base plate further into the ground. If the angle of the plate changed, he lost his trajectory and elevation. Despite this, he kept up a continuous fire.'

The attacking party now swarmed up to the perimeter of the strip with the Captain of the Boat Troop in the forefront, and when in decent range let fly with small arms and 66 mm light anti-tank rockets. There was now some return fire from a bunker to the side of the strip, but this was generally ineffective. The assault group now split into pairs to deal with those aircraft that were not already wrecked, but as David reported: 'It was a bloody big strip and they had a lot of ground to cover. It's not as if the planes were parked in one neat row. They were all over the strip. And all the time the boys were running against the clock.' Five planes were destroyed using the explosive charges that they had brought with them.

The Pucara was the tallest of the aircraft. As they approached each plane, one bloke would give the other a leg up onto the wing.'

According to one account, the charges were all placed in similar locations on the aircraft, so minimizing the possibility for 'cannibalization', using the parts of one to repair another.

Other planes were simply shot up from close range, but in some instances a few bullet holes did not seem conclusive enough, so grenades were used as well. One man reported emptying a whole magazine from his M16 into a Pucara in short bursts, and watching the shards of perspex fly off into the air. Yet towards the end of this brief orgy of violence one plane remained stubbornly intact. So whilst Captain Hamilton provided cover, Trooper Raymond 'Paddy' Armstrong sprinted up to it, and in a scene reminiscent of Paddy Mayne's exploits half a century earlier, smashed and ripped parts off it. With *HMS Glamorgan* still dropping shells on enemy positions, including fuel dumps and stores, the signal was given for retirement.

Only one man of the assault team had so far suffered any injury, having taken a shrapnel splinter in the leg, but as they retreated a mine was detonated and the unfortunate Corporal Bunker, already slightly injured in the South Georgia operation, was blown off his feet.

'Bomb disposal experts' are dropped into the sea close to the *Queen Elizabeth II*, to search the ship after a bomb threat. The incident would later form the inspiration for a feature film. The SAS would use identical 'air to ship' drop tactics in the Falklands.

As the man with the leg wound recalled: 'I was beginning to feel faint from loss of blood and was consequently told to head back… with two others [including Corporal Bunker]. Just off the airstrip we heard Spanish voices, at least four or five, shouting some 50 metres towards the settlement. I opened fire… and put down some 60 rounds in the direction of the voices. Two very pained screams were the only reply.'

The teams were successfully extricated by helicopter and regained *Hermes* without further mishap. For this and other actions, Major Delves received the Distinguished Service Order, while Captain Hamilton was personally credited with four aircraft, which contributed to his award of a Military Cross. In all, the raiders had accounted for 11 aircraft: six Pucaras, four Turbo-Mentors, and an Argentinian Coastguard Skyvan. Remarkably it was later discovered that the enemy garrison had numbered 114, but only one platoon of Marine conscripts had been left watching the field that night. About a quarter of the Argentine ground attack planes based on the Falklands had been destroyed in less than half an hour.

TAKING THE FALKLANDS

The 1 May 1982 saw not only the opening of a very public bombardment of the Argentinian positions on the Falklands by naval guns, Vulcan bombers, and Harriers, but the covert commencement of the land campaign by the SAS. It was G Squadron, led by 'Fablon' Houston, which would play the major role in this clandestine operation, and Houston was an ideal candidate for the job since he owed his nickname to his apparent ability to mould his body to any surface when under fire. The first 16 men of G Squadron, in four patrols, were landed from Sea King helicopters of 846 Naval Air Squadron in the early hours, and were followed by a further six patrols over the next two days. As added security, they were dropped several miles from their final observation posts, and

marched unseen to their positions carrying with them everything they needed, including observation equipment and transmitters.

By daylight, the men dug shallow scrapes and camouflaged them with peat or netting, and kept still and silent. Where possible, these uncomfortable holes were lined with plastic, but they were inevitably cold and damp as rain came down from above and water seeped in from below. There was seldom a chance of hot food and even urinating was potentially perilous as give-away clouds of steam rose into the frozen air. It was, as Tony Geraghty put it, the ultimate 'Costa Hypothermia'. One veteran described the experience: 'When I came back in off the first OP, I reckon I was in quite a bad way. I'd lost quite a bit of weight, my legs were shaky, I was getting bad headaches, and I was feeling dizzy all the time. I didn't tell anyone… and I felt a lot better after some decent food and proper rest. My Bergen on that one must have been 120-140 pounds, easily. We had all the OP kit, we had first aid gear, batteries, ammunition, rations, water, and we all had the warm clothing, but we… needed it, no two ways.'

Nevertheless, an effective network of observation was getting into position even as the naval war hotted up with the sinkings of the *Belgrano* and *Sheffield*. Eventually there were two watches on Port Stanley, and others on Bluff Cove, Cow Bay, Port Salvador, San Carlos Water, and Goose Green. The watches around Port Stanley were particularly vital since part of the Argentinian defence plan was to keep back a reserve in this area, and ferry them by helicopter to any threatened point. SAS activity in locating the helicopters and calling in air strikes against them was of strategic importance. On West Falkland, Port Howard, Pebble Island and Fox Bay were all placed under observation.

Meanwhile the SBS, dubbed by the SAS the 'Shaky Boats', turned their attentions to beaches and potential landing grounds. The combined work done by all these patrols was invaluable, for even those who saw nothing helped to establish weak spots in the Argentinian defence. Amongst the toughest jobs were those done by SAS Captain Aldwin Wight and Sergeant Joseph Mather. Wight's observation post on Beaver Ridge overlooking Port Stanley was maintained continuously for 26 days during appalling weather, and resulted not only in a clear picture of the Argentine dispositions but an air strike against enemy helicopters. Mather watched Bluff Cove and Stanley for a total of 28 days, and was forced to move his post several times, his only protection against detection being the 'skill and stealth' of his patrol, as his Military Medal citation pointed out.

The picture that was built up of the enemy showed them to be inexperienced, though well equipped, and present in large numbers. There was a later complaint that the information provided by the SAS did not percolate through to all the troops who needed it, and there was a very unfortunate friendly fire incident in which the SAS shot Sergeant Hunt of the SBS. Yet according to Peter de la Billière, then Director SAS, this was not so much the fault of the men on the ground as much as a drawback of 'the system', and it was 'a measure of their skill and discipline that none of the patrols was found or captured.' One SAS officer would later admit that he thought that there

Damaged Argentine training aircraft at Pebble Island, Falklands, 1982.

were simply too many Special Forces operatives and patrols in the same space. This was essentially the point of view noted by Robert Fox, then working for BBC Radio: 'There were so many men from the specialised forces, the SAS, SBS, and Mountain and Arctic Warfare Cadre, that they almost seemed in danger of tripping over each other. As Martin Osborne of 3 Para remarked, the "naughty boys" club of SAS and SBS seemed to have been let out of school.'

Despite such quibbles, SAS participation in the Falklands had so far been stunningly successful, and casualties thankfully light, until after dark on 19 May disaster struck. That evening D Squadron was preparing to take part in the landings on East Falkland, and was being transferred by helicopter from *HMS Hermes* to the assault ship *Intrepid*. This routine operation was almost complete when the last elements, including much of Mountain Troop, boarded the Sea King for the five-minute journey. The helicopter reached *Intrepid* without event, but was forced to hover for some time as another craft was still being cleared from the flight deck. At this point, the engine suddenly banged loudly and the Sea King dropped out of the sky about 400 feet into the icy water. It has since been assumed that this was the result of a catastrophic bird strike.

It was a small mercy that the helicopter was not falling so fast as to incapacitate instantly all those aboard, and some men were able to struggle free as the passenger compartment flooded. So it was that 10 survivors including the co-pilot gained the surface and were left bobbing around in a small dinghy. One of the crew had activated a rescue beacon, and a flare was fired, but it was still some time before a rescue helicopter was on the scene, with the result that those in the water were exhausted and half frozen. One man was winched clear before a small rescue vessel closed in and plucked the remainder from the sea. They were revived aboard *HMS Brilliant*, and later sent back to Britain. Amongst their number was an SAS man

who had now survived a total of three helicopter crashes; with typical grim humour the Regiment now nicknamed him 'Splash'. Twenty men were never recovered, a total which made this tragedy the regiment's worst single loss since the Second World War. The dead included many good men, some of them victors of the Pebble Island raid. Amongst the casualties were Squadron Sergeant Major Gallagher, veteran Staff Sergeant P. Curass, holder of the Queen's Gallantry Medal, and G Squadron Sergeant Major M. Atkinson. Also killed was Trooper Raymond 'Pucara Paddy' Armstrong. Even Corporal Bunker's luck had finally run out.

NIGHT RAID

Just two days after the accident, British troops began coming ashore on East Falkland, the relatively safe landing of the paratroops in Operation Sutton being in part attributable to the preparatory efforts of SAS and SBS Special Forces. Yet the SAS had one other service to perform in support of the landings: a diversionary raid, which was one of several designed to distract Argentinian attention from the main location at San Carlos Water, and cause further confusion and demoralisation.

The now depleted D Squadron was airlifted from *Intrepid* and deposited east of Goose Green to launch a noisy demonstration supported by *HMS Ardent*. The force committed was about 40 men, under the direction of Major Delves. To keep the enemy guessing, and the helicopter transport out of harm's way, the party was dropped in more than one place some miles away from their target areas, and so had to march under cover of darkness, carrying all their necessary kit. To be convincing as a large body, and so fool the enemy into believing that a single squadron was in fact a battalion-size invasion, this equipment would include GPMGs, mortars, Milan launchers, plenty of ammunition, and the latest American-made anti-aircraft missile, the Stinger. It was an impressive array of hardware, but it made a journey of the better part of 20 hours a serious test of endurance.

D Squadron succeeded in getting into position in the low hills north of Goose Green without discovery well before dawn. On cue they began to fire Milans, and hose down the Argentine positions with streams of bullets from the machine guns. Rather than remain static, the little teams moved about, attempting to give the impression of greater numbers. On balance, it seems unlikely that this noisy fusillade delivered from long range claimed many Argentinians, but this was not the point of the exercise. By forming a screen of fire they made it far less likely that the garrison would venture out in the direction of San Carlos, and interfere with the work of the invasion force. The enemy returned fire, but remained effectively pinned to the locality. By this means, 2 Para were given the opportunity to leave the beaches relatively unmolested, and advance in the direction of Sussex Mountain.

Having performed their task without loss, D Squadron broke off the engagement at first light and began to melt away to the north, where they were expected to link up with friendly forces. It was thought that the excitement was over, but at this vulnerable moment, in broad daylight on open terrain, a Pucara ground attack aircraft appeared and began to buzz the retreating figures. One of the SAS, since identified as 'Kiwi', fixed the battery unit to his Stinger, calmly stood up, and launched his rocket. The Pucara disintegrated, much to the relief of the firer: the episode being greeted with huge enthusiasm by members of 2 Para who had now reached vantage points, and were able to get a grandstand view. More Pucaras appeared later, and sensibly stood off so as not to meet the same fate as their colleague. Other Stingers missed their intended targets, but even though the weapon was new, it was acting as a significant deterrent to the slow-moving Pucaras.

With surveillance established, the enemy garrison shaken by raids, a bridgehead created by the main force, and a route open to Darwin and Goose Green, much had been achieved. Yet the British ships in 'Bomb Alley' were still very vulnerable to air strike, especially from the Exocet missile, and the main prize of Port Stanley appeared a distant and formidable obstacle. Late May saw many vessels damaged, and *Ardent, Antelope, Coventry*, and *Atlantic Conveyor* all sunk. The sinking of *Atlantic Conveyor* would be particularly significant to the troops ashore, for a vital reserve of helicopters were lost with her, and the troops were left no option but to walk. 'Yomping', meaning to march long distance across inhospitable terrain, soon entered the national vocabulary.

The British strategy evolved into what was essentially a two-pronged ground advance on Stanley, to the north, via Teal Inlet with 3 Para and 45 Royal Marine Commando, and south, with 2 Para via Darwin and Goose Green. At Goose Green on 28 May, 2 Para took on more than twice their number, and defeated the 2nd and 12th Argentinian Regiments. Close assaulting their trenches with small arms and grenades before capturing 1,100 of the enemy, it was a remarkable performance, but cost 17 dead, including the Paras' commanding officer Colonel H. Jones. There was controversy, not only about the conduct of the battle, but how the SAS information on the Argentinian garrison could apparently have been so hopelessly inaccurate. It may be that there was some under-estimation, but it is equally probable that additional bodies like enemy naval and headquarters personnel were discounted, and that the Para officers were not going to be discouraged by greater enemy numbers. In any event, Goose Green eliminated a potential threat on the British flank, and delivered another body blow to enemy morale.

The SAS had likewise done much in the face of odds, but it had not been without cost. In addition to the dead of the disastrous helicopter accident there had been wounded and hypothermia cases who had required evacuation. D Squadron in particular was much under strength and it was certainly not yet possible to fly passenger aircraft into the Falklands. Nevertheless, there was a typically inventive, not to say hair-raising way, in which the Regiment could rectify the difficulty. Men from B Squadron, hitherto held in reserve at Hereford, were flown out from the UK to Ascension Island, and here transferred into C130 Hercules. These rear-loading transport aircraft were then taken over the Task Force, and the SAS reinforcements parachuted into the ocean to be picked up by *HMS Andromeda* and deposited safely at San Carlos Water.

The procedure was described in detail by Soldier 'I': 'Alongside me in the womb of the aircraft sat several newly badged members of the regiment. I thought of the strict precision and ruthless timing required by our plan. I looked at the fresh faces of the new recruits… A few minutes later, with arms outstretched and convulsing like a cat coughing up a fur ball, I had cursed and struggled my way into my dry suit. I stowed my fins where they would be easily accessible for fitting once I was in the water. Next the parachute. It was already adjusted to my personal measurements, so it was simply a matter of hoisting myself into the harness – not an easy task in the cramped passenger space of the Hercules. Finally, I strapped a distress flare to

The Regiment's cemetery, located in the grounds of St Martin's, Hereford, by the road out of town towards Ross-on-Wye.

my wrist… The tail gate ramp was now fully down. I gazed out over the airdrop pallets crammed onto the ramp itself curving away into space and into the Atlantic swell 800 feet below… The plane bucked in slight turbulence, and I realised with a palpitating heart that this was the moment of truth. I took a deep breath, clipped on my reserve and moved into position… "Red on. Green on. Go!" screamed the dispatcher, slapping me on the back. Automatically I leapt into space, forcing my right hand down on top of my reserve to improve my exit stability. For an instant I was carried violently forward in the blast of the Hercules slipstream. Then I felt the reassuring tug of the parachute harness and the profound relief that the canopy had deployed… I saw I was directly above the dull bluey-grey shape of *HMS Andromeda*… I pulled down violently – too violently – on my steering toggle. This caused air to spill out of my canopy. I began to oscillate through 180 degrees. I spiralled downwards, my rate of descent increasing. I swung back and forth, but at least I managed to clear the ship… Now I was conscious only of the water rushing up to meet me.'

After half an hour in the water, hands and face numb with cold, like a 'piece of battered flotsam', Soldier 'I' was plucked from the South Atlantic by a Marine boat handler. Soon he was on his way to make up the numbers of D Squadron. Others, like Frank Collins, had the disappointment of turning back to Ascension from the drop zone. Faulty parachutes had caused the loss of some equipment and it was feared that men would meet the same fate if the drop was continued.

Amazingly, the possibility of flying B Squadron straight into Stanley in an attempt to bring the war to a swift and spectacular conclusion was also considered. Fortunately, common sense prevailed and a slightly longer, but, in the end, more certain route to victory was followed. This was not to say that the remaining SAS actions of the war were not imaginative, nor without serious risk.

LAST ACT

The next task was the significant problem of Mount Kent. This daunting natural feature, 1,400 feet high dominated the approaches to Stanley, and could, if left alone, have provided the enemy a vantage point from which to observe and dangerously hinder the British advance. A four-man patrol of G Squadron was already ensconced on the hill, but now SAS Lieutenant Colonel Mike Rose put forward a plan for its denial to the enemy. The result was that following further reconnaissance, D Squadron was now lifted forward and deposited on Mount Kent in advance of the Marines, to harry, watch,

ambush, and generally make life uncomfortable for any Argentinians who decided to take up position there.

D Squadron occupied Mount Kent for a week, some of that time out of contact with friendly forces, and made it difficult for the enemy to determine what was going on in the area, let alone turn the hill into a defensive position. On the night of 27 May, an Argentine patrol entered D Squadron's zone of control, a fact that was swiftly apprehended by Captain Hamilton, and a fire fight ensued. The startled enemy beat a hasty retreat, but not before the SAS had taken a prisoner. The next night another incursion fared

Memorial tablets on the wall of the regimental burial ground, Hereford. The quotation is repeated from the verse on the regimental clock, which also lists the names of the fallen. Those who leave the Regiment alive and well are said to have 'beaten the clock'. Warrant Officer Lawrence 'Lofty' Gallagher joined the Regiment in 1968 from the Royal Engineers, becoming a member of Boat Troop.

It was he who raised the Union flag on South Georgia in 1982. Sergeant Sid Davidson joined the SAS in 1973 and served in both Dhofar and Northern Ireland; like Gallagher he was killed in the disastrous helicopter crash in the Falklands on 19 May 1982. Captain Hamilton MC was killed at his observation post near Port Howard on West Falkland.

little better, and was again seen off by a brisk return of fire. According to one account, some of the opposition were actually Argentinian Special Forces, brought in by helicopter specifically to deny Mount Kent to the British. They had not realised that the SAS had beaten them to it. On 30 May, 42 Commando began to arrive, and what had been a tenuous Special Forces toe-hold behind enemy lines was turned into a regular lodgement, and a stepping stone on the way to Port Stanley.

On 1 June, Hamilton and his men scored a significant success, ambushing yet another Argentine patrol sent to winkle them out, wounding three of the enemy and capturing another five. As the possibility of victory hove in sight with the beginning of June, old inter-service and inter-regiment competitiveness began to become something of an issue. As Robert Fox put it: 'The SAS and other specialist units were carrying out what is called with the euphemism of military jargon, "aggressive patrolling" in the high ground around Port Stanley, though they do not appear to have penetrated the garrison in the port successfully. They talked of "malleting" everything in sight, as the paratroopers wanted to "banjo" the enemy, and the Marines "welly" them. There was some irritation at the SAS activities as orthodox forward infantry patrols from many of the Marine and paratroop officers, who felt that their units had perfectly suitable patrol companies for the job. With their peculiar command structure and direct access to the UK, the SAS did not come under the orders of either Brigade Commander on the Falklands.'

The Paras and the Marines naturally vied for honours, and the field was made all the more crowded by the arrival of the Guards and G urkhas from the *QE2* and *Canberra*, which had been stood off until the dangers from the air had been perceived to be reduced to an acceptable level. The SAS, who had done much good work, were in danger of being overlooked, at least partly because of the very covert nature of their operations. It was perhaps these circumstances which led Lieutenant Colonel Mike Rose to decide to visit D Squadron on Mount Kent in person, and to take the extraordinary step of taking war correspondent Max Hastings along with him to report on the proceedings. The publicity *coup* almost backfired when it became apparent that a gun battle was still in progress less than a mile from the press visit. Major Delves explained that this was only a little local difficulty, which would be 'sorted out' in the morning. With the SAS moving onto Murrell Heights, 3 Para preparing for Mount Longdon, and the Guards now squaring up for a set piece action against Mount Tumbledown, Delves' prediction was proved only marginally over optimistic.

Even so, with the arrival of strong conventional forces, including artillery and light armoured fighting vehicles at an ever tightening Stanley perimeter, the opportunity for imaginative SAS action was decreasing. One possibility examined was an SAS and SBS co-operative venture to raid Stanley from the seaward side using scuba divers. This did not materialise, perhaps as it was accounted an unnecessary risk, and in the event much SAS activity was now focused on the potentially better hunting ground of West Falkland Island. Here, there were Argentinian garrisons relatively untouched, and if these could be infiltrated, observed and discomfitted, it was possible that they might be convinced to give up the struggle without an expensive and potentially bloody new campaign.

The SBS had already investigated much of the coast of West Falkland, and had drawn the conclusion that many of the settlements were unoccupied. In the first week of June, the SAS relieved the G Squadron observers who had already spent much time on the 'other island', and upped their contribution by redeploying part of D Squadron in small patrols. These would later be backed up by B Squadron, which would be present only for the last days of the war. One of the tasks begun, but not complete at the end of the war, was the attempted location and elimination of a suspected enemy observation post at Mount Rosalie, which it was thought was acting as a guide to incoming attack aircraft from the mainland.

At the forefront of the renewed effort on West Falkland was the irrepressible Captain Hamilton, who now occupied a two-man observation post overlooking Port Howard from a distance of about two kilometres. Here there were thought to be about 800 of the enemy, still in very belligerent mood. At dawn on 10 June, everything went horribly wrong: Hamilton became aware that the enemy had succeeded in surrounding his post, and there seemed no option but surrender or an attempt to fight his way out. In the ensuing exchange of fire, Hamilton was mortally wounded. To give his colleague a chance to escape, Hamilton kept shooting as long as possible. 'Fonz', the signaller with him, made a break for it, and might have got further but for the fact that he ran out of ammunition. He was captured and held in the cellar of a sheep shearing shed until the end of hostilities. For this unselfish action, and his previous exploits at Pebble Island and on Mount Kent, Hamilton was awarded a posthumous Military Cross.

The next SAS action of the Falklands War was a distinct contrast to this covert activity on West Falkland. On the night of 13 June, it was planned that 2 Para would attack and seize Wireless Ridge, one of the last significant obstacles around Port Stanley. Since the enemy were well dug in and present in numbers, it was decided that any help the Paras could receive in the form of an SAS diversion would be very welcome. Accordingly a daring plan was hatched by which two troops of D Squadron, a troop of G Squadron, and a handful of SBS men would raid Wireless Ridge from the

seaward end. This would be supported by naval gunfire and by comrades who would add to the confusion by descending from Murrell Heights and firing missiles and machine guns into the hapless enemy.

This was the plan, but the event only narrowly avoided disaster. Owing to bad weather, the raiders from the sea had to use assault boats rather than helicopters. As the Rigid Raiders passed the hospital ship *Bahia Paraiso*, an alert watch detected them and search lights were turned on. This was the signal for every Argentinian within range to open fire. Particularly dangerous were a battery of 20 mm anti-aircraft cannon which swept the water like a scythe, and threatened to smash the small craft to matchwood. As one veteran put it, the 'world opened up'. Discretion being the better part of valour, the raiders were swung round, but not before a number of rounds had slammed home. All four boats were hit and damaged, two of them seriously. Fortunately all craft escaped and there were no fatalities, but four men were injured and one boat, holed below the waterline, later sank.

The happy corollary to this sad farce was that the Paras' attack on Wireless Ridge proceeded like clockwork. It was stalled briefly when an enemy 155 mm gun found their range and three men were killed, but was pushed forward again with skilful support by four tanks of the Blues and Royals. The Paras were able to gain Wireless Ridge, and took a number of prisoners whilst the rest of the defenders melted away down the hill. An attempted Argentinian counter-attack from the direction of Moody Brook was smashed by British artillery. The next day a patrol of G Squadron added significantly to the enemy discomfiture by calling down fire on the rear of the enemy positions at Tumbledown. By now the Argentinian 'defensive horseshoe' around Stanley was well and truly breached. The war had only hours to run before surrender.

SAS AT WAR

Saddam Hussein's Iraqi Army invaded the small oil rich state of Kuwait on 2 August 1990, throwing the Western world into turmoil. Saudi Arabia was under threat, Western airlines hastily withdrew their aircraft and personnel, and many Western civilians became hostages – a 'human shield' against retaliation. American and British forces were rapidly moved to the Middle East in Operations Desert Shield and Granby respectively, but months of painstaking diplomacy followed. President Bush and Margaret Thatcher were fully committed to action to reverse Iraqi aggression, but work was need to secure international consensus and a viable and durable military coalition of both Arab and Western States. Only with this kind of support could Saddam be ousted from his conquest without Kuwait becoming a 'new Vietnam'. Other problematic areas included the possibility of Iraqi chemical and biological warfare, and the potential ecological disaster of burning oil fields.

At the outset, it appeared that the job of the SAS would be gaining information on hostages held by the Iraqis, and very probably hostage rescue. About 800 British subjects were in Kuwait at the time of the invasion and a similar number in Iraq itself. To make matters worse, these were spread out, and included women and children. In the event, the hostages were released in December partly as an Iraqi bid to swing international opinion, partly as a result of the endeavours of Edward Heath and other brokers. The possibility of a full scale war, and Iraqi air, missile, and chemical weapons appeared to be next in the potential order of priorities. As political manoeuvres continued, British Special Forces began to gather.

The Gulf would see the biggest deployment of Special Forces and the largest single SAS operation since the Second World War. By December 1990, there were about 700 British Special Forces troops available, including the Royal Marine Special Boat Service, signallers, headquarters staff, and some RAF personnel, but by far the most significant contribution would come from the SAS. The Regiment would send over 300 men, including A, B, and D Squadrons of the regular 22 SAS, plus a dozen reservists of R Squadron. G Squadron, which had recently trained with D Squadron in the area, had been rapidly moved to the United Arab Emirates at the outbreak of trouble, but was withdrawn back to Hereford at Christmas forming a last reserve.

PREPARATION FOR WAR

On an individual level, preparation was thorough, but the detail of clothing and equipment varied from man to man. Corporal Chris Ryan described his uniform and kit as follows: 'I was dressed, like the rest of the guys, in regular DPMs (disruptive pattern material combat fatigues). We'd also been issued with lightweight, sand-coloured desert smocks which—unbelievably – dated from the Second World War. I had worked my silk escape map into the waistband that held the drawstring of my trousers, and taped the twenty gold sovereigns given us for E&E (escape and evasion) purposes onto the inside of my belt. On my head I was wearing a German Army cap – a souvenir of my Alpine guide course – and on my feet a pair of brown Raichle Gortex-lined walking boots, with well insulated uppers and soles, which I'd also acquired in Bavaria at a cost of more than £100. On my hands I had a pair of green aviator's gloves, made of fine leather. As useful extras I had two shemags I'd bought in Abu Dhabi. One was very light coloured, and I'd made vain efforts to darken it by dyeing it in tea. The other was thicker and more suitable, being oatmeal and purple, with the design favoured by the special forces in Oman. In my right arm I was cradling my chosen weapon, a 203, which I had fitted with a makeshift sling made of nylon para cord.'

Ryan readily admitted that he had become

'obsessed' with the need for ammunition, and accordingly the only rations he carried on his belt kit were biscuits, putting the rest of his 24 hour emergency ration pack into the Bergen to make more room for bullets. Altogether, he loaded up with 12 magazines of 28 rounds and about 90 loose rounds including a few for armour piercing. More food went into a sandbag, mainly 'boil in the bag' ready meals, and tinned fruit. Not being a great tea drinker, and thinking there would be little opportunity for fires, he left his brew kit behind to save weight and space. He later felt this was a mistake. Superstition prompted him to tape a couple of 'lucky' coins to his metal identity tags.

Cameron Spence recorded that he was limited to 80 lb of kit and rapidly came to the conclusion that pretty well everything should be customized to his own requirements. He approached the seamstress at Hereford and had extra thick pads sewn into the elbows and knees of his combats. Extraneous zips were replaced with quick-release velcro and field dressing pockets were added to the calves of the trousers. She also made a pair of sand gaiters to go over the boots. He similarly decided that the issue webbing was inadequate to the task. He ordered his own from a specialist

company in Devon: 'I drew up what I wanted on the back of a fag packet.' The resultant rig was not unlike a Second World War battle jerkin in desert camouflage material, and included special pouches on the chest for grenades, medical dressings, and cylume sticks. He purchased his own shoulder holster for the issue Browning 9mm pistol, and a 20 round magazine.

Interestingly, the contents of his Bergen were also personalised to the extent that he included a miniature short wave radio, for BBC World Service listening, his own specification escape and evasion kit in a tobacco tin, and customized water containers. These last consisted of plastic bags with nozzles, flexible enough to mould themselves to the shape of the inside of the pack. Perhaps the most extraordinary item he stowed away was a condom intended to keep water out of the muzzle of his M16. Slings for weapons are often frowned upon in the Regiment on the basis that if a weapon is carried it should be at the ready, not on the shoulder. Even so, some men improvised slings out of the ubiquitous rubber bungee, tying rifles to their backs.

Other features of preparation concerned the possibility of wounding, capture, or death. As protection against nerve gas, the men were ordered to take Nerve Agent Pre-Treatment or 'Naps' tablets. For pain control, there was an issue of one syringe and two syrettes of morphine per man; the syrettes being generally hung around the man's neck on paracord. Precautions against capture included the provision of gold sovereigns for barter, silk escape maps, and compasses. A 'blood chit' leaflet in English and Arabic was carried, explaining that anyone helping the bearer would be well rewarded.

For 'iso-prep' or Isolation Preparation, each man was asked to give a few personal details that no one other than his closest friends and relatives might know. This would make it more difficult for the enemy to glean information by

Nocturnal Gulf War tank action.
Defence Picture Library

The unpredictable Iraqi
desert, 1991. This wadi had
been dry for years, yet during the Gulf War it was a fast
flowing river. The SAS Land
Rover is armed with a GPMG
and stowed with two spare
wheels, at least one missile,
helmets, and a mass of
smaller items.

faking a prisoner's release and then questioning him again. Only when an SAS man had these personal facts repeated back to him would he know that he was in a genuine debriefing. General 'cover-stories' were not given out, it being assumed that name, rank, and number were all that could be expected of a captive under the relevant conventions. Even so individuals dreamed up their own stories to spin out time: some of the more popular included being members of air crew rescue teams, medics stranded with wounded, and the like. Finally, each man was allotted a code number to be used in case of his death and 'next of kin' letters were written and sealed.

SCUD HUNTERS

A final ultimatum regarding Iraqi evacuation of Kuwait expired on 15 January 1991, and with the commencement of the air and Scud campaigns on 17 January action was imminent. The advent of the Iraqi Scud missile offensive was critical to the role in which the SAS was eventually used. Saddam cunningly targeted Israel, even though she was not actually engaged in the war, in the hope that she would retaliate. In this event there would be dire consequences for the coalition, for few Arab states would wish to be seen to be fighting on the same side as Israel against an Arab neighbour, whatever her recent violations of international law. The destruction of the Scud threat was thus of strategic importance and became the primary target of Allied Special Forces activity.

It soon became apparent that the Scuds were being launched from two areas in the west of Iraq, not far from the Jordanian border. The task of dealing with them was made more difficult by the fact that the Scud Boxes were so far behind enemy lines and besides concentrations of Iraqi forces. On the plus side, it was soon to become apparent that the Allies had overwhelming air power, and that if well handled, Special Forces and aircraft could complement each other in action.

Top, Detail of the Colt AR-15, 5.56 mm, rifle. Designed by Eugene Stoner, an employee of Armalite Incorporated, the AR-15 is a light weight high velocity small calibre rifle well adapted to contacts up to 400 metres, with a 20 or 30 round box magazine. First examined by the Infantry Board in 1958, the weapon was adopted in the US as the M16 a few years later. It saw use with the SAS in Borneo in the 1960s, and thereafter has usually been carried by the Regiment in preference to the standard issue Army weapons. It was in particular evidence in the Falklands and the Gulf. A shortened Commando version is favoured for Northern Ireland.
Middle, Detail of a Russian AK 47 assault rifle. The famous gas operated selective fire 7.62 mm Soviet AK 47 was designed during the Second World War, and appeared as a prototype in 1947. Simple and very effective, it has been used both against and by the SAS. As a potential enemy weapon, the AK 47, and its derivatives, AK 74, AK 101, AKS, feature in training. The original model weighed 4.3 kg and had a 30 round box magazine and knife bayonet.
Bottom, (Left) the Browning 9 mm High-Power semi-automatic pistol. First produced in Belgium in 1935, the 'Millie' was an advanced design used by Germany, as well as Britain, Canada, and other countries after the invasion of Western Europe in 1940. A reliable and handy weapon, the Browning has been widely used by both the SAS and the British Army in general. Perhaps its most useful feature is its 13 round magazine. (Right) Introduced as early as 1929, the Walther PP is a 7.65 mm semi-automatic pistol with a double action trigger mechanism. Intended for police work, the Walther was widely used by the SAS in undercover situations, particularly during the 1970s and 1980s. Since then, the Glock and SIG handguns have become more popular, having a larger round and bigger magazine capacity, though they are more difficult to hide.

The planned deployment of the SAS would see almost three whole Squadrons committed. B Squadron's contribution would be three road watch patrols, each of eight men, positioned on the North, Centre, and South of the Iraqi Military Supply Route. The primary objective of these B 10, B 20, and B 30 patrols would be to relay information on road movements to air units and other Special Forces, who would do the main job of destruction. A and D Squadrons would fulfil the classic desert raiding role, very much as formulated by David Stirling against German air power half a century before. Using light vehicles, explosives, and machine guns they would traverse the desert seeking out targets for the bombers and fighters, cutting communications, and destroying targets of opportunity.

Each of A and D Squadron's vehicle mounted convoys consisted of two self-sufficient half squadron groups, each of about 30 men. They put a total of four fighting columns into the field. Each fighting column comprised eight 110 Land Rovers, a Unimog mother support vehicle, and four motorcycles. The main fighting vehicle was the Land Rover or 'Pinkie', so called because SAS Desert Land Rovers had, from time immemorial, been known as Pink Panthers, due to the particular shade of their desert camouflage originally applied.

Though each column was based on a Troop, it was decided that a senior Mobility Troop man should be included in every column, making sure that each had a fully trained mechanic. Two Land Rovers formed a double sized eight-man patrol, and each Land Rover acted as a platform for a three or four man crew. For the purposes of the operation, one man served as commander, one as driver, and a third as gunner. The spare man was primarily a motorcyclist, but, owing to the stress caused by long distance desert two wheel driving, was frequently swapped around with other members of the group. The two vehicle eight-man

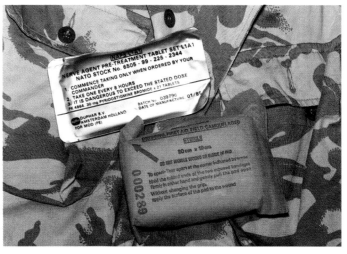

Top, The kevlar combat helmet Mark 6, seen with desert camouflage cover and goggles, was favoured in the Gulf.

Bottom, The Dressing, First Aid, Camouflage, and the infamous Nerve Agent Pre-Treatment tablets, as used in the Gulf. Some members of the Regiment did not trust the NAPS tablets, and never took them, others have cited them as a contributory factor in Gulf War Syndrome. A desert camouflage smock is seen in the background.

patrol group was so organised that it also included within its ranks at least one weapons expert, one demolition man, a medic and an Arabic speaker. It was therefore possible to break the half squadron into two or three, and still be able to function under all eventualities. The Unimog had a basic crew of two, driver and co-driver, and since it was primarily a supply vehicle was usually attached to a pair of Land Rovers for protection.

The primary armament of the Land Rovers varied. Some mounted .50 Browning heavy machine guns, some Mark 19 grenade launchers, and some Milan missiles. According to Mike Curtis, D Squadron's Mountain Troop half column of four Land Rovers was equipped as follows: vehicle 1 – GPMG at front, double GPMG at rear; vehicle 2 – GPMG at front, .50 Browning at rear; vehicle 3 – GPMG at front, double GPMG at rear; vehicle 4 – GPMG at front, Mark 19 at rear. Also carried inside the Land Rovers and Unimog were the men's personal weapons, and a selection of other surprises for the enemy. Most important amongst these were the Milan missile, and single shot disposable 94 mm and 66 mm anti-tank weapons which would allow dismounted engagement of armour and soft skinned vehicles. The possibility of

SAS fighting column personnel in the Iraqi desert. An armed Land Rover, motor cycle, and Arab coat are in evidence. Note also the diversity in webbing and footwear.

including little fast attack four wheelers and Giat 20 mm cannon with columns was also considered, but both were left behind. The former were declared unsuitable for boulder fields, whilst the 20 mm guns were felt to be a liability due to a lack of night sights, and electrical feed which might prove difficult to maintain.

According to Mike Curtis, packing the Land Rover was an art in itself: 'Everything had a place: the Milan missiles; bar mines [anti-tank]; boxes of explosives, including L2 [anti-personnel] and white 'phos' grenades; 7.62 link for the gimpies; 5.56 link for the Minimis (contained in green plastic boxes, each holding 200 rounds); boxes and boxes of 5.56 cartons for the Armalites and M203 bombs; ten Jerry cans of water; ten Jerry cans of fuel; two weeks supply of compo [rations] per man; boxes of hexamine [cooker fuel] ; Bergens; five complete sets per man of NBC (nuclear, biological and chemical) suits, including gloves, boots and associated items; and boxes of batteries and gas bottles for the spyglass and MIRA thermal imager.'

Helmets were sometimes strapped to the side of the Land Rover where there were also container brackets. On the front of each vehicle were mounted six smoke dischargers, a set of three either side, worked by a switch on the dashboard. Some crews attached an 'escape' Bergen containing water, food, and a sleeping bag to the front by means of a rubber bungee, which could be cut loose in the event of emergency.

Finishing touches included the naming of vehicles and the provision of artistic embellishments. Mike Curtis recalled that his vehicle was named *Pegasus* because the crew were all ex- Parachute Regiment. A plastic covered picture of Madonna went on the side by way of a mascot. Cameron Spence's vehicle was named *Tarakiwa*, after the Maori God of war. Later, many Land Rovers would be embellished

The ill fated Bravo Two Zero
patrol just prior to their insertion behind enemy lines.
The faces of the survivors are
obscured. The casualties were,
left, Robert Consiglio MM,
a former Royal Marine
Commando, centre, Trooper
Steven Lane MM, a former
Royal Engineer, and right,
Sergeant Vince Phillips, who
previously served with the
Royal Army Ordnance Corps.

Next page, SAS Land Rover
and support vehicles cross
the stony billiard table of
North Western Iraq, 1991.
Inhospitable terrain often
made concealment difficult.

with the silhouettes of crossed out vehicles and other hardware on their right front wings, mementos of enemy equipment destroyed.

BRAVO TWO ZERO

B Squadron's road watch teams were inserted towards the end of January, but it was soon apparent that all was not well. The South road watch was put in by Chinook helicopter, but as he alighted, the NCO in charge could see nothing but a featureless gravel plain. There was nowhere to run and nowhere to hide; as an observation point the location was useless. Taking a courageous, and with the benefit of hindsight a perfectly correct decision, he re-boarded the helicopter and the eight men were brought out again. The experience of Central road watch was similar. On arriving at the agreed point by vehicle, they found nowhere to lay up, and deemed the risk of compromise too great to remain. Having called in an air strike on a nearby radar station they beat a hasty retreat. Though posted as missing for a time they made it back safely.

North road watch exited from the interior of a Chinook fitted with an extra fuel tank, almost 200 miles from friendly territory, on 22 January. With the arrival of the eight-man patrol 'Bravo Two Zero' would commence one of the bravest,

Milan launcher on top of an SAS Land Rover, Iraq, 1991. The Milan missile gave sufficient fire power to take on targets like Scud launchers, convoys, and strong points at a distance.

if ultimately most futile, episodes in SAS history. From their night time drop point in a dried up river bed, they had to march several kilometres in shuttles to their agreed cache point. Arguably they were attempting to carry far too much, the patrol leader Sergeant Andy McNab estimating the load per man at 209 lb. This included not only four Minimi Light Machine Guns and four Armalites with 203 grenade launchers, but a 66 mm rocket each, ammunition, hand grenades, claymore mines, radio equipment, food, clothing, and heavy Jerry cans of water. Nevertheless, they reached the Laying Up Point successfully.

Not long afterwards, they discovered they were near neighbours of an Iraqi Anti-Aircraft battery, positioned to protect the very road convoys they had come to observe. Compromise by a young goat herd quickly followed. The patrol packed up and moved off, leaving only their claymores behind, only to run into first a civilian bulldozer, then enemy Armoured Personnel Carriers and trucks. The patrol immediately engaged these with 66 mm rockets, and the Iraqis spilled out of their carriers whilst the machine gun turrets returned fire on the SAS. It was, as McNab was only too happy to admit, extremely frightening to be a foot patrol up against armour and infantry in strength. Even so Bravo Two Zero gave a good account of themselves: 'Everybody was getting the rounds down. The Minimis were fired in bursts of 3-5 rounds. Ammunition had to be managed. Two 66s were fired at the truck and found their target. There was a massive shudder of high explosive. It must have been very demoralising for them.' The patrol then did the totally unexpected, rushing forward in bounds, attacking their attackers. According to McNab's recollection, this apparently suicidal manoeuvre allowed a grenade to be thrown into the back of one of the carriers, and the other to be driven off. Chris Ryan's version differs in detail and plays down the heroics, but either way they survived this first contact.

This initial success in the face of disaster only succeeded in attracting yet more attention. The patrol came under fire from anti-aircraft guns and was pursued by lorry-borne infantry. Bergens were discarded and Bravo Two Zero made their escape northwards as best they could. In the darkness and confusion of crossing the Military Supply Route, the patrol was split up into two groups. Communications were not working, sleeping bags were lost, clothing insufficient. The mission had deteriorated into escape and evasion – a simple struggle for survival. In this the main enemy was not so much the Iraqis as nature – cold, exhaustion, and dehydration.

By the night of 26 January, the smaller group was in deep trouble. It had been snowing, and they were reduced to hiding in waterlogged ditches, and ruts created by tank tracks to avoid detection. All three were beginning to suffer from hypothermia. As they stumbled along, Sergeant Vince Phillips lost contact with his two colleagues. They were unable to relocate him and he died of exhaustion. Not long afterwards, one of the remaining two was captured attempting to find a vehicle in which they might make a more speedy and comfortable escape. This left just Corporal Ryan, who decided that his best course of action would be to follow the Euphrates towards the Syrian border. The river banks were more populated, but at least the terrain was less exposed and, though he had only two biscuits, at least he could be sure of water. On 30 January, he walked across the border, feet blistered, nails lifting, after walking for seven nights. He thus became the 'one that got away', earning himself a Military Medal.

The larger remnant of Bravo Two Zero had problems of their own. They avoided several enemy vehicles, but were soon suffering from the cold and risked brewing drinks and huddling together for warmth. Tactics were 'thrown to the wind'. Turning adversity to advantage, they

Heavily stowed Gulf War 'Pinkie' with GPMG. This vehicle retains its roll bars. One account states that these were removed on some Land Rovers helping to lower the silhouette, but increasing the danger to the crew in the event of an accident.

replenished their water bottles with snow. McNab described how his smock and shemag froze to his body. They too pressed on towards the North West and, crossing a road, managed to hijack a taxi which they later had to abandon at a checkpoint.

Nearing the border near Al Qaim, they ran into more concentrations of the enemy and were compromised again. On 27 January, an unequal running battle broke out and Trooper Bob Consiglio was shot and killed whilst covering the escape of his comrades. McNab and a slightly wounded comrade were captured soon afterwards. When finally cornered, McNab had run out of ammunition, and was cowering in a drainage ditch just a mile or two from the safety of Syria. The last two men swam a river, but the intense cold of waterlogged clothes drained their last reserves of strength. Trooper Steven 'Legs' Lane was now dying of hypothermia. His comrade alerted nearby Arab civilians in the hope that Lane would receive medical attention, but was himself captured. Bravo Two Zero had lost seven of its eight men, three dead, and four captured.

FIGHTING COLUMNS

On 20 January, the four fighting columns of A and D Squadrons went over the border into Western Iraq, crawling around enemy positions at night, using Passive Night Vision Goggles, pocket scopes, and satellite navigation equipment. For the most part this went smoothly, though at least one team of A Squadron had problems traversing the anti-tank berm at the border and was forced to drive up and down looking for a crossing place. Tiredness, cold, and rough terrain were as much hazards as the enemy. Track rods broke, drivers fell asleep and shunted into the backs of the vehicles in front, and men huddled up in inadequate clothing. NBC suits, Norwegian shirts, bobble hats, and whatever came to hand were quickly put on.

Before daylight the columns would make a few dog legs to cover their tracks, then they would lay up, covering the vehicles with camouflage nets, putting mines on likely approaches, setting sentries, and placing support weapons to cover the best arcs of fire. Camouflage nets could be put up in various ways, but perhaps the best was to make a form of garage using the support poles, so that the Land Rover could be driven out in double quick time. Cameron Spence, with A Squadron, described the setting out of the defence zone as a 'science in itself'. The vehicles were placed within a radius of about 150 metres and the Milans, as the primary anti-tank weapons, placed first. 81 mm mortars came next, providing scope for bombardment out to several kilometres. The

Opposite, **SAS Squadron Ambush, Western Iraq, February 1991. Though the main focus of A and D Squadron fighting columns was destroying Scud missiles, communications and targets of opportunity were also engaged. Much of the action was at night when full advantage could be taken of hand held thermal imagers, surprise, and 'shoot and scoot' tactics. During daylight, the enemy were more able to pursue and make numbers count. A particularly difficult action occurred on 21 February when one of the A Squadron columns became involved in a running battle which lasted for several hours, and covered a distance of over 20 miles. There were at least three exchanges of fire as the column attempted to ambush enemy vehicles, and were then chased across the desert.**

The illustration shows a sniper who has been acting as sentry to the column directing his comrades onto Iraqi vehicles. The sniper, foreground, wears the SAS smock with soft drill cap and five-pocket chest harness. His weapon is the Accuracy International 7.62 mm bolt action sniper rifle, adopted as the L96A1 by the British Army. This features an aluminium frame, weighs 6.2 kg, and has a ten round magazine. Using a Schmidt and Bender telescopic sight and two stage trigger, it is expected to be effective against individuals at 600 metres, and produce useful harassing fire up to 1000 metres. It is seen here with its alloy bipod folded up under the barrel.

The motorcycle outriders were commonly used for reconnaissance and communication, yet were often heavily armed. This man has a 66 mm Light Anti-Tank Weapon secured to the handlebars of his machine, and an Armalite rifle with M 203 grenade launcher slung across his chest. The US designed, breech loading, single-shot 40 mm M 203 is effective to about 400 metres – total weight when combined with the rifle is about 5 kg. The helmet is the Helmet Combat, GS Mark 6 worn with a camouflage cover secured by means of a drawstring around the base of the helmet. Britain had sold off her stocks of desert camouflage uniforms prior to the Gulf War so there was a rush to produce the jacket and trousers in Lightweight Desert DPM during the autumn of 1990. It is said that difficulties in production, including a wrangle between the Ministry of Defence and a contractor in the north-west of England over the type of buttons, were the cause of insufficient supplies of desert camouflage during the campaign. The result was that the SAS, like many other units, went to war in a mixture of desert and ordinary temperate disruptive pattern material camouflage.

The Land Rover or 'Pinkie' is armed with a pintle mounted GPMG by the commander's seat and a 40 mm Mark 19 automatic grenade launcher in the rear compartment. The Mark 19 was first developed by the US Navy for use in Vietnam, and is an air cooled blow back weapon capable of being used with a variety of rounds including high explosive anti-personnel. It is effective to about 1600 metres and fires from a linked 20 or 50 round belt. Though it has a cyclic rate of about 350 rounds per minute, it may also be used to fire single shots. Smoke dischargers on the front of the Land Rover helped to conceal movement in the event of a compromise. The heavily stowed vehicle was capable of supporting a four-man patrol for about two weeks before resupply. By the time the fighting columns returned to Allied lines, the Land Rovers had covered upwards of 1500 miles in enemy territory. *Painting by Richard Hook.*

machine guns and other weapons came last, providing interlocking and enfilading fire.

In theory, food was prepared three times a day, and the boil in the bag rations approximated to breakfast, lunch, and dinner. In practice, cold, the appearances of the enemy, and limited time meant that much 'stew' was eaten, a euphemism for throwing the contents of various packets together and cooking the concoction with whatever spices or sauces were available. Eating was usually perfunctory, hanging about too long could mean blown sand in the food. For sleep, the 'green maggots' or sleeping bags would be unrolled and laid beside or even under vehicles.

First contact with the enemy was made by an A Squadron group. Four Iraqi artillerymen, including at least two officers, drove up to a laying up point in a Russian GAZ car. An officer got out, as Peter Crossland reported: 'The Iraqi approached, a look of bewilderment on his face. His head-dress, a blue beret, had the Iraqi eagle emblem badge on it… Not until he was three metres away did he realise we were the enemy. Mel swung up his rifle and fired. Nothing happened. Automatically he dropped to one knee to clear the weapon stoppage, and by doing so he cleared my line of sight… I fired and the man fell dead. With that, the world erupted as everyone else opened fire.' Three of the enemy were killed and one prisoner and some maps were taken.

By 24 January, SAS patrols had penetrated the southern Scud Box, and despite snow and fog, were patrolling the desert, reporting sightings of enemy troops or strong points back to Allied Air Forces. Though equipment was available to 'paint' targets with laser equipment during actual attacks, it was far more usual just to take co-ordinates and report them by radio. Two days later, a patrol reached the main Military Supply Route and was able to observe traffic on the road. Such was the Allied control of the air that it proved possible to fly in supplies and spare parts and to

General Sir Peter de la Billière, Commander, British Forces Middle East and former Director SAS in desert combat uniform.

evacuate a few men whose vehicle was unserviceable and had to be destroyed. One re-supply was particularly welcome, bringing a heap of Arab overcoats bought by a thoughtful store-man in a bazaar in Saudi Arabia. These came in grey, dark brown, and fawn, sometimes often with gold braid, in one size, extra large. After supply, empty fuel containers and other rubbish was dealt with in a novel way, being soaked with petrol, and then fitted with an incendiary charge set to go off a couple of hours after the column's departure.

Remarkably, one re-supply was carried out by ground vehicles. For this purpose, a temporary E Squadron was established, consisting of ten four-ton trucks protected by six armed Land Rovers crewed by men of B Squadron. The whole ad hoc outfit was commanded by a Major, who coolly drove into Iraq, found the rendezvous and drove back out again without serious mishap.

On 29 January, one of the D Squadron fighting columns was compromised and attacked by Iraqi troops. Fortunately, the sentries were alert and met the assault with concentrated machine gun fire. As the enemy pressed the attack, the crews of the British vehicles let fly with their .50 calibres and other support weapons, tearing their own camouflage nets to pieces, but halting the Iraqis. The decider was the Mark 19 grenade launcher, as Mike Curtis relates: 'On one of the other wagons, Jim Dalton opened up on the far ridge with the M19… The effect was awesome. He fired several bombs in quick succession and seconds later the explosions echoed down the wadi… The impact of the M19 had won the fire fight and changed the entire complexion of the battle. From being on the back foot, 17 Troop now had a breathing space, but the Iraqis were certain to regroup and come back at them. The main priority for the lads was to get out of the wadi.'

One SAS Lance-Corporal was hit and badly wounded, but at least ten enemy and two vehicles were claimed. As the conflict was broken off, it became clear that the Unimog support vehicle and seven men, including the wounded man, were still in the wadi. Though it was not immediately known, this resourceful little team had abandoned their own transport and succeeded in escaping in a damaged Iraqi Dodge Jeep. Much to the puzzlement of the Saudi border guards, all made a safe return to Allied lines.

The other D Squadron group also had a contact which was bravely contested by a Milan team. A Land Rover raced in, picked them up and retired. An A Squadron team managed to destroy some cables, but were pursued by Iraqi vehicles and one of their Land Rovers turned over, resulting in one man injured. On 9 February, there was another contact in which a fire fight resulted in the loss of a Sergeant Major. He was believed dead, but was actually captured by the enemy, and though given the usual harsh interrogation and beatings, survived the war.

It may have been the suspicion that SAS teams were being detected by communications towers, plus their growing confidence, which now encouraged them to turn their attention to fixed positions. At Victor Two, A Squadron took on a protected radio tower by means of demolition charges. The tower was destroyed but the team was engaged in a vicious fire fight as they made

John Major, British Prime Minister, meets and greets the 'desert rats' in the Gulf. Like the RAF, the preliminary efforts of the SAS helped to make the ground war a resounding success.

Next page, SAS ground troops direct air strikes in Kosovo.
Defence Picture Library

their escape, as Peter Crossland relates: 'The red and green hornets were everywhere, dancing in the amazing fireworks display that only war can create. The crack and thump of a thousand rounds whistled all around us. Tracer rounds flew past at incredible speed, then stopped suddenly as they hit a hard surface. I heard zip, zip, zip as hot lead buzzed my arms, my legs and my head… Amid this chaos the fire support group were fighting desperately to extract themselves.'

Over the next few days, SAS teams cruised the desert and destroyed seven communications stations along the route of the old Baghdad to Amman highway. Towards the end of this successful operation, an A Squadron team got caught up in a series of running combats. During an ambush on the enemy on 21 February, the Regiment suffered its fourth and final fatality. Lance Corporal David Denbury, a motor cycle outrider, was hit in the chest and killed. Like several of his colleagues, Denbury was awarded the Military Medal.

There has been much debate over the SAS role in the Gulf, most particularly as to how many Scuds they actually destroyed and how many they allowed Allied air power to find. It seems unlikely they actually destroyed very many, but the mission had been significant. Communications were disrupted, large areas of the Scud Box denied to the enemy, and launches rendered less effective as a result. Perhaps most importantly it was clear to the Israelis that Britain and America took the Scud threat seriously and were doing something about it, without upsetting their Arab Allies. In this respect, the contribution of the SAS was invaluable and may have effected the course of the war. As the Allied Commander in Chief put it to Sir Peter de la Billière: 'continued firing of Scuds' could have resulted in the 'dismantling of the carefully crafted coalition.'

BOSNIA AND KOSOVO

Though information on the activities of the Regiment is understandably in short supply for recent years, one of the latest accounts states that it is current practice to keep one squadron as a Counter Terrorist or 'Special Projects' team, and thus be available for domestic crises such as aircraft hijacks. A second squadron is on standby for significant events overseas (and will therefore have spent much time in the Balkans), whilst the third and fourth will be training, though one of these is regarded as the backup for significant events. Interest is doubtless maintained in Northern Ireland. Ever more sophisticated specialist skills and technology make their appearance. Attached Engineers and Signallers, for example, make use of the latest in bomb disposal, computers, and electronic countermeasures. Tours average about six months before squadrons are rotated.

The shifting political landscape of the former Yugoslavia has provided much of the Regiment's recent work at the end of the 20th century. Slovenia and Croatia declared independence in 1991, and Bosnia erupted into violence the following year. D Squadron were in Bosnia by 1992. According to Cameron Spence's account, some patrols were insinuated disguised as ordinary signallers, armed with ordinary SA 80 rifles, reverting to civilian dress and Armalites as required. Their major tasks were to map out where the front lines, if any, actually were, then to penetrate Muslim enclaves such as Maglaj, and report back conditions and any evidence of atrocity.

It was in Bosnia in 1994 that the Regiment suffered its last but one fatality when Corporal F.M. Rennie was shot by Serbian Chetniks. The same year, in the same country, the Regiment provided the bodyguard for Prime Minister John Major during a visit. Since then, SAS have gathered intelligence and sought out war criminals for the attention of the international war crimes tribunal.

More recently it has been reported that the SAS were involved in the move to evict Serbs from Kosovo. Newspaper reports have suggested that a mission was planned on 11 June 1999 to fly two patrols into Pristina airport ahead of the Russian arrival. The load of the aircraft, however, which included Land Rovers and motorcycles, shifted, and caused the pilot difficulties. An emergency landing was attempted and as the Hercules came in, it clipped a building and crash landed. Most of the team got out, but one was trapped and badly injured. As a source reported in *The Sunday Times* put it: 'Military historians will eventually have a field day with the Kosovo conflict.'

SAS LEGACY

The SAS was one of the first truly Special Forces and maintains a reputation throughout the world for quality in its chosen calling. Exchanges and joint exercises take place with other Special Forces, in particular the US Delta Force, but also European units like Germany's GSG 9. Members and ex-members of the SAS are in constant demand for the training of other forces, and as bodyguards for politicians and celebrities. It is almost expected that when soldiers leave the Regiment they will do one or the other.

Yet the significance of the SAS is much more than this. When it was formed, the Regiment marked a small but important evolutionary step in strategy and tactics. David Stirling suggested that not just small units, but individuals, count in campaigns. Moreover, such troops could be given strategic objectives. A few determined and daring men, given the right training, the right equipment, and the right spirit are capable of making a contribution out of all proportion to their numbers and cost. So it is that the SAS lay little store by the 'thundering herds', but go like 'pilgrims… always a little further'.

The windows of the regimental chapel at St. Martin's Hereford commemorating the campaigns from North Africa to Iraq. Four spaces remain for future engagements.

Military Illustrated is the leading monthly
military history magazine in the English language.
Since its inception, it has built up an unrivalled
reputation among military historians, enthusiasts,
collectors, re-enactors, and military modellers
for authoritative articles, primary research,
rare photographs, and specially commissioned
artwork spanning the entire history of warfare
from ancient to modern – including the most
popular periods such as World Wars Two
and One, Napoleonic Wars, and ancient and
medieval combat.

Copies of the magazine are available on
newstands and in specialist shops or can
be obtained directly from the publisher
on subscription from:

Military Illustrated
45 Willowhayne Avenue
East Preston
West Sussex
BN16 1PL
Great Britain
Tel: 01903 775121

BIBLIOGRAPHY

Armstrong, N.A.D., *Fieldcraft, Sniping and Intelligence*, 1940.

De La Billière, P., *Looking For Trouble*, 1994.

Bruce, P., *The Nemesis File*, 1995.

Chant, C., *SAS in Action*, 1997.

Collins, F., *Baptism of Fire*, 1997.

Connor, K., *Ghost Force*, 1998.

Crawford. S., *SAS Gulf Warriors*, 1995.

Crossland, P., *Victor Two*, 1996.

Curtis. M., *Close Quarter Battle*, 1997.

Darman, P., *Weapons and Equipment of the SAS*, 1993.

Davies. B., *SAS: the Illustrated History*, 1997.

Devereux, S., *Terminal Velocity*, 1997.

Dewar, M., *Weapons and Equipment of Counter Terrorism*, 1987.

Farran, R., *Winged Dagger*, 1948.

Ford. S., *One Up. A Woman in Action with the SAS*, 1997.

Fowler, W., *SAS. Behind Enemy Lines*, 1997.

Gander. T.J., *Jane's Military Training Systems*, 1990.

Geraghty, T., *Who Dares Wins*, 1993.

Harrison, D.I., *These Men are Dangerous*, 1957.

Hipkiss, J., *Unarmed Combat*, 1941.

Hoe, A., *David Stirling*, 1992.

Hoe, A., & Morris, E., *Re-enter the SAS*, 1994.

Hunter, G., *The Shooting Gallery*, 1998.

Jane's Infantry Weapons
(various editors and editions)

Kennedy. M.P., *Soldier 'I', SAS*, 1989.

Manuals (Official), *Notes on Camouflage and Concealment*, 1939; *Forest, Bush and Jungle Warfare Against a Modern Enemy*, 1942; *Fieldcraft*, 1944; *Sniping*, 1951; *Close Quarter Shooting*, 1961; *General Purpose Machine Gun*, 1966; *66 mm Anti Tank Rocket*, 1970.

McCallion. H., *Killing Zone*, 1995.

McNab, A., *Bravo Two Zero*, 1993.

McNab, A., *Immediate Action*, 1995.

Nicholson, F., *Married to the SAS*, 1997.

Ramsay. J., *SAS The Soldier's Story*, 1996.

Ryan, C., *The One That Got Away*, 1995.

Scholey. P., *The Joker: 20 Years Inside the SAS*, 1999.

Seymour, W., *British Special Forces*, 1985.

Simpson. J., *Biting the Bullet*, 1996.

Spence, C., *Sabre Squadron*, 1997.

Spence. C., *All Necessary Measures*, 1998.

Sutherland, D., *He Who Dares*, 1998.

Thompson. J., *War Behind Enemy Lines*, 1998.

Weale, A., *The Real SAS*, 1998.

Whiting. C., *Death on a Distant Frontier*, 1996.

Young, B.A., *The Artists and the SAS*, 1960.

SAS DIRECTORY

Museums

The SAS likes to protect its privacy – secrecy is vital to its success and survival, therefore any directory of sources will be short. That said, there are places to visit to learn about the history of the Special Air Service. Until its media success in the 1980s, the SAS had its own museum at the Duke of York's Headquarters in the King's Road, Chelsea, London, but this has now been closed for some years.

Two museums in London do possess SAS material and objects:

Imperial War Museum, Lambeth Road, London SE1 6HZ (tel: 020 7416 5000);

National Army Museum, Royal Hospital Road, Chelsea, London SW3 4HT (tel: 020 7730 0717).

It is also possible to visit the Regimental chapel at St. Martin's Hereford, located just outside the town centre on the road to Ross-on-Wye.

Books and Research

The Regiment is more difficult than most to write about as it confirms and denies nothing – secrecy helping to maintain its aura of invincibility. Many accounts of SAS actions are written or spoken under pseudonyms. Where material of this sort has been quoted in the text then these cover names have been left as given, but the accounts have been compared to other sources describing the same events. The result has been to reveal that one SAS memoir of recent years is, in fact, complete fiction, but it also helps to cofirm the basic truths of other works.

Many of the recent books on the Regiment are available through libraries and book shops. It is worth recommending a few mail order stockists who may have some of the rarer volumes:

Ken Trotman
Unit 11, 135 Ditton Walk
Cambridge CB5 8PY
(tel: 01223 211030)

Athena Books
34 Imperial Crescent, Town Moor
Doncaster, South Yorkshire DN2 5BU
(tel: 01302 3229130)

Caliver Books
816-818 London Road, Leigh-on-Sea
Essex SS9 3NH
(tel: 01702 4739860)

Ray Westlake Military Books
53 Claremont, Malpas, Newport
South Wales NP9 6PL
(tel: 01633 854135)

The museums mentioned above both have libraries containing specialist material which may be used by appointment for research. Many papers relating to the Second World War are now available from:

Public Records Office
Ruskin Avenue, Kew, Surrey.

Records for individuals are at present only accessible to next of kin. Inquiries should be directed to:

The Army Records Centre
Bourne Avenue, Hayes
Middlesex UB3 1RF.

INDEX

ACKNOWLEDGEMENTS

Several people have helped with the
research for this book, but not all can
be thanked in print. I should like to
make particular mention of the staffs
of Lancashire County Library and
the Imperial War Museum, as well
as Ted Neville of TRH Pictures and
David Reynolds of the Defence Picture
Library, for their invaluable help with
reference and illustrations. Thanks too
to Tim Newark for his patience and
for convincing me that the project
was possible.